CREATION
AND THE
PATRIARCHAL
HISTORIES

Orthodox Christian Reflections on
The Book of Genesis

by Patrick Henry Reardon

Ancient Faith Publishing
Chesterton, Indiana

CREATION AND THE PATRIARCHAL HISTORIES:
Orthodox Christian Reflections on the Book of Genesis
© Copyright 2008 by Patrick Henry Reardon

All Rights Reserved

Published by   Ancient Faith Publishing
                    A division of Ancient Faith Ministries
                    P.O. Box 748
                    Chesterton, IN 46304

Printed in the United States of America

ISBN 978-1-888212-96-9

With immense gratitude to
Father Paul Suda,
by whose anointing hands
our family was received into the Holy Orthodox Catholic Church,
July 15, 1988,
the Feast of St. Vladimir of Kiev,
in the Millennium Year of the Kievan Mission.

CONTENTS

INTRODUCTION

⁂

Because Genesis is found at the beginning of the Bible, no one is to be blamed for starting his Bible-reading with Genesis. This is perfectly logical.

Many of us Christians, nonetheless, knew a good deal of the content of Holy Scripture before we ever got around to reading Genesis. There is a logic in this case too, for the simple reason that many of us, perhaps most of us, were introduced to Jesus before we were introduced to the full biblical account of history. That is to say, we were familiar with the Gospels before we knew much about Genesis.

Nonetheless, when we started reading the Bible in a systematic way, we generally started with Genesis, presuming that there must be some reason why this book is the first one found in Holy Scripture.

The origins of the world and more especially of the human race occupy the opening pages of Genesis, which provide the theological suppositions, not only of the ensuing chapters, but of the biblical story as a whole. These suppositions are Creation, especially that of man in God's image, the structure of time (prerequisite for historiography), man's relationship to God, the entrance of sin into the world, and God's selection of a specific line of revelation that will give structure to history. This history begins with the call and life of Abraham and continues in the stories of his offspring, in the cycles of Isaac, Jacob, and Joseph. By the end of Genesis, these offspring of Abraham have arrived in Egypt, and the Bible is ready to start Exodus. In short, Genesis is concerned with the origins of our race and the beginnings of salvation history.

Much of the material in Genesis is arranged in a pattern of ten generations, indicated by the famous "begat" passages that have discouraged so many readers on their first time through the book. These generations (*toledoth* in Hebrew) begin already in 2:4: "These are the generations of the heavens and the earth when they were created" (RSV). That is to say, *God* began the generations. The second occurrence of this formula is found in 5:1, which lists the early offspring of Adam. The third list is in 6:9–10, introducing the family history of Noah. His offspring are listed in 10:1, those of Shem in 11:10, and Terah in 11:27. This brings us to Abraham, the father of Isaac, whose progeny are listed in 25:19, and Ishmael, whose offspring are found in 25:12. Of Isaac's two sons, Esau's generations are noted in 36:19 and Jacob's in 37:2.

The Book of Genesis does not stand alone. It is the first of the "five books," the *Chumash*, of the Mosaic Law, the *Torah*, or Pentateuch, "the five scrolls." This means that its narrative in Genesis continues seamlessly in the story of Exodus, parted only by the physical necessity of being composed on a separate scroll. When Genesis is cited in the New Testament, therefore, the ascription usually refers to "the Law" or "Moses."

Indeed, the composition of Genesis, as well as of the Torah as a whole, is credited to Moses, a persuasion that testifies to the unity of the work. This traditional ascription of the work to Moses is found everywhere in Jewish and Christian literature.

Was Moses in fact the author of the Book of Genesis? Surely not in the sense that Moses composed every last syllable of the Torah; even the strictest interpreter of this question recognizes that the account of the death of Moses in the last eight verses of Deuteronomy could hardly have come from Moses himself. Other verses also indicate a later hand, such as the comments that "the Canaanite was then in the land" (12:6), and "there was yet no king in Israel" (36:31). In addition to this internal evidence, there is also the biblical account of a discovery of "the Law of the Lord" in the Temple at Jerusalem during the time of King Josiah in the late seventh century BC. From very early times this document has been identified (by St. Jerome, for example), as a whole or in part, with the Book of Deuteronomy. If this identification is valid—and the original form of Deuteronomy had a separate history unfamiliar to those who discovered it in the late seventh century—this is strong evidence that the arrangement of "five books" is considerably later than Moses.

Over the past several centuries various textual historians have devised sundry theories, according to which the material in the Torah, including Genesis, came from various pre-existent literary sources preserved for centuries at the different shrines in the Holy Land. Those that espouse these theories call attention to the different names by which God is invoked in different parts of the Pentateuch, different names for the same people and places, and different styles of narrative and theology.

The present writer is not much impressed by these theories. Variations of style and theology do exist in the Pentateuch, of course, including Genesis, but not, I think, with the consistency that justifies a recognition of different literary sources, certainly not sources that can be readily identified. After several centuries of these hypothetical theories with respect to the literary sources of the Pentateuch, we actually know precious little about them for sure. In particular, it seems to me, these theories have contributed almost nothing to a better exegesis of the Sacred Text.

For this reason, the present writer will be content to regard Moses as the author of Genesis, this ascription being understood in a general sense that affirms the theological and literary unity of the Pentateuch. This unity I will be everywhere at pains to affirm and demonstrate. By speaking of the Mosaic authorship of the Pentateuch, however, I do not intend to discount the later editorial work of Ezra and others in the formation of the Sacred Text that has come down to us.

This canonical text has been handed on to us by the apostolic churches chiefly in the Greek form, the Septuagint. This is the text of authority in the Church.

This affirmation does not mean, however, that the Greek text necessarily represents an "original" text better than the traditional Hebrew manuscripts preserved by the Jews. Often enough it may, but that is not what we mean when we speak of the canonical authority of the Greek. In our affirmation of the Septuagint's canonical authority, it is obvious that we Orthodox Christians do not limit divine revelation to an original text or "autograph" composed by the biblical author himself. We cannot logically affirm the canonicity of the Septuagint except by postulating the Holy Spirit's guidance of the entire development of the biblical material throughout the centuries that link the prophets with the apostles. After all, no reasonable Christian will claim divine inspiration for Isaiah's

Greek translators and simultaneously deny that inspiration to Isaiah himself!

Thus, in a given passage, we are not obliged to choose between the inherited Hebrew and Greek readings. It is quite legitimate to accept both, each of them representing a different stage in the development of the biblical tradition. This approach, which I think both reasonable and respectful, will be taken in the present book, where both the Christian and Jewish copies of Genesis are consulted.

The question of the canonical status of the Septuagint in the Orthodox Church, moreover, prompts two other observations, which I hope will prove useful.

First, the Septuagint's canonicity is not absolute. It is rooted in the respect commonly shown for this version in the New Testament, but its historical application has been far from rigid. The tradition of the Christian biblical manuscripts shows, rather, a considerable diversity in textual selections. The most notable example, I suppose, is the Book of Daniel. After Origen, in his famous *Hexapla*, placed Theodotion's translation of Daniel in a parallel column with that of the Septuagint, Christian copyists compared the two renderings and decided that they much preferred Theodotion!

Thus, in spite of the traditional and venerable authority of the Septuagint in the Church, Theodotion's translation of Daniel came to predominate among Christian manuscripts. For instance, his version was adopted as the Danielic text of the Byzantine liturgical lectionary. Similarly, Theodotion's translation of Daniel, not the Septuagint's, was the version translated into almost all the other ancient versions used by the Church: the Peshitta Syriac, both the Boharic and Sahidic Coptic, the Latin Vulgate, the Ethiopic, the Armenian, the Arabic, and the Slavonic. (The exceptions are the Syro-Hexaplar and the Vetus Latina, both translated from the Septuagint.) So great was the dominance of Theodotion in this respect that the ancient Septuagint version of Daniel almost disappeared from history, not a single copy of it being known until the discovery of the Chisianus Codex in 1772. These plain historical facts should preclude any rigid interpretation of the Septuagint's canonical status.

Second, when Holy Scripture is quoted in the present volume, the quotation will normally be taken from *The Orthodox Study Bible*, which is based on the Septuagint and was published during our editorial process. Sometimes exceptions are made, but these will always be indicated. Likewise, for the sake of consistency, I will also refer to the biblical books by the names they bear in the Septuagint, which are preserved in *The Orthodox Study Bible*.

GENESIS IN THE GOSPEL PROCLAMATION

The Apostle Paul, treating the connection between the Torah and justification by faith, poses the following question to the Christians at Rome: "Do we then make void the law through faith?" And resoundingly he answers, "Certainly not! On the contrary, we establish the law" (Romans 3:31).

Paul's answer to the question is, I submit, pretty much unintelligible if we think of the "law" as a corpus of rules to be observed. How would the law, understood in that sense, be established by faith?

The context in Romans, however, belies such an approach, because Paul immediately cites the Torah itself to explain what he means: "What then shall we say that Abraham our father has found according to the flesh?" (4:1). The "law" that Paul has in mind here in Romans is not a corpus of rules; it is, rather, the Torah in its integrity, including the historical narrative. Indeed, it is specifically to the narrative of the Torah that Paul directs our attention: "For what does the Scripture say? 'Abraham believed God, and it was accounted to him for righteousness'" (4:3; Genesis 15:6). That is to say, Paul finds in Abraham himself an example, perhaps *the* example, of a man justified by faith. It is clear to Paul that the Torah itself proclaimed the doctrine of justification by faith (Romans 4:9; Galatians 3:6). In short, the Torah taught the same thing the Gospel teaches. There was no dichotomy between Law and Gospel on the matter of justification. Both taught the identical doctrine.

For Paul, moreover, the Gospel is what provides the proper basis for understanding the Torah itself. The Gospel is the key to the Law, providing the correct understanding of that literature. Paul's new interpretation of the Law differs from that which he had espoused before his conversion to Christ, and that difference is the Gospel.

But what is true of the Torah is true also of the Prophets. For this reason, we see Paul going to the prophetic books of the Bible and finding there the same teaching that he proclaims in the Gospel—namely, Habakkuk's declaration (2:4) that "The just shall live by faith" (Romans 1:17; Galatians 3:11). There is no canonical distinction here. Just as the Gospel is the key to the Torah, so it is the key to the Prophets.

Likewise, what is true of the Torah and the Prophets is true also of that third part of the Hebrew Scriptures, the Writings, the *Ketubim*. Let us return to that same fourth chapter of Romans, where "David also describes the blessedness of the man to whom God imputes righteousness apart from works" (4:6). Paul goes on to quote the words of the Psalter: "Blessed *are those* whose lawless deeds are forgiven, / And whose sins are covered; / Blessed *is the* man to whom the LORD shall not impute sin" (Romans 4:7–8; Psalms 32 [31]:1–2). Thus, Paul finds the proclamation of the Gospel in this third section of the Hebrew Scriptures, as well as in the Torah and the Prophets.

In finding the Gospel message in all three sections of the Hebrew Bible, Paul's thesis is identical with what we find in Luke, where the risen Jesus says to the Church, "These *are* the words which I spoke to you while I was still with you, that all things must be fulfilled which were written in the Law of Moses and *the* Prophets and *the* Psalms concerning Me" (Luke 24:44). And then, writes Luke, "He opened their understanding, that they might comprehend the Scriptures" (24:45).

It is important to see that this correct understanding of the Old Testament Scriptures is the context of the Great Commission to preach the Gospel to all nations, which follows immediately in the Lukan narrative (24:46–49). That is to say, the New Testament teaches that the proclamation of the Gospel is inseparable from the correct understanding of the Torah, the Prophets, and the Writings. The very beginning of the Gospel proclamation is "Thus it is written" (24:46).

The Old Testament is not a body of writing extraneous to the Gospel. On the contrary, those Scriptures are integral parts of the Gospel. Without that Old Testament, the Gospel we Christians preach is not the genuine article. When we declare "that Christ died for our sins," it is always "according to the Scriptures." When we proclaim "that He was buried, and that He rose again the third day," it is invariably "according to the Scriptures" (1 Corinthians 15:3–4).

We Christians hold that the pursuit of either Testament on its own, apart from the other, is theologically unwarranted. The Old

Testament cannot be correctly understood in its fullness, we contend, without the New Testament, nor can the New Testament be correctly understood apart from the Old. Both together form a single, theologically indivisible canon of divinely inspired literature.

Thus, in the first Christian sermon recorded in Acts, Peter invokes "the God of Abraham, Isaac, and Jacob" as the God of the Christian Gospel (3:13). Stephen, in his own presentation of the Gospel, begins by announcing that "the God of glory appeared to our father Abraham" and then runs through much of the history of the Old Testament, all the way to Solomon, before he so much as mentions the name of Jesus (7:2–59). We find this same appeal to the Old Testament in the Gospel as preached by Philip (8:32–33) and by Paul (13:15–37).

If we turn these considerations to Genesis specifically, it is not difficult to see various ways in which the themes from this book are incorporated into the proclamation of the Gospel. For example, this incorporation is obvious with respect to Creation, a doctrine from Genesis everywhere incorporated into the Church's message to the world (e.g., 2 Corinthians 4:6). Indeed, much of the opening section of the present book is devoted to a Christian understanding of Creation.

This incorporation of Genesis into the Gospel is manifest likewise in the stories of Adam (Romans 5), Noah (1 Peter 3), Abraham (John 8, James 2, Romans 4, Hebrews 7), Jacob (Acts 7), and sundry others. It will be everywhere my intention, in the pages of this book, to read the Book of Genesis through the lens of the Christian Gospel.

CREATION & LITERATURE

Probably the most serious challenge that modern thought presents to the faithful reading of the Book of Genesis is the theory of random evolution, which logically discounts the theology of the opening accounts in the book. If it is the case that the existence of all things, including the human being, came from the blind juxtaposition of chemical components, then the world itself—to say nothing of the human being that lives in it—has no intrinsic meaning. It would not be true, on this hypothesis, that "the heavens declare the glory of God." This is the reason that so much of the early part of this commentary will focus on the implications of the biblical doctrine of Creation.

To counteract the baneful influence of the theory of random evolution, many apologists have elaborated a contrary theory more faithful to the actual facts provided by science: intelligent design. This perspective takes account of the irreducible complexities within nature that are mathematically impossible to explain by a process of random development. Indeed, those who espouse the theory of evolution, especially in the biological form of it bequeathed by Darwin, have in proving their theory a task far more difficult than that of someone who would attribute the faces on the side of Mount Rushmore to the weather conditions in South Dakota.

What is missing in the theory of random evolution is the acceptance of the obvious: The world around us contains massive evidence of an effort to convey information. This intent to convey information was obvious to the ages of faith, which is the reason for the thesis popular back in those days: "The *fool* says in his heart, 'There is no God.'" From Moses to the present day, believers have always insisted that the created world is a book chock full of divine revelation—a complex message from God, the very proclamation of His eternal Word. The world is, in short, a colossal piece of writing. This is the reason the construction of the world appears as the first component in God's "second work" of literature—the Bible.

For this reason, it seems proper to introduce the Book of Genesis by showing how the biblical doctrine of Creation is related to the world of literature and theology. These two fields become inseparable, obviously, in the Book of Genesis, which is the beginning of both biblical literature and biblical theology. It is significant, then, that the biblical story begins with *genesis*, a Greek word meaning "origin." Accordingly, I will argue the thesis that the biblical doctrine of Creation is the presupposition of all biblical literature, not only in a material sense but also formally, meaning that the created world is God's original exercise in grammar construction. We should start, I think, by examining the way in which the created structure of the universe forms the first "text," the original *grammata* of the Christian faith. Just what do we mean when we say—with the whole Christian Tradition—that the world is "written" work?

It is passing curious, and perhaps deeply significant, that writing began exactly where the story of Abraham began: at the southeast end of the Fertile Crescent. Our earliest examples of "writing" come from near the end of the fourth millennium before Christ and were bequeathed to us by a race that historians, taking their cue from the traditional name of the place, chose to call Sumerians. All historical study of the Bible properly begins where script itself began, in that ancient region where the Tigris and Euphrates flow out to the Persian Gulf. Thus we say that Sumerian was our first written language, a language vastly older than Hebrew and the radical source of all literature. We begin our study of Genesis, then, with what we learn at Sumer.

Now it is a most interesting feature of these Sumerian texts that, though we are sure they represent a written language, we cannot decipher the first several centuries of them. Only the Sumerian texts from some five or so centuries later are we able to *read*.

The reason for this is very simple. From this later period, about the middle to the end of the third millennium BC, we happen to possess parallel texts written in a very ancient Semitic tongue, Akkadian, and we are able to use this latter language, much more firmly within the grasp of linguistic history, to make a reasonable reconstruction of later Sumerian vocabulary and grammar. Except for these Akkadian parallel texts, we would not be able to read Sumerian at all. There remain, nonetheless, those several earlier centuries of texts written in Sumerian that we are still unable to read.

With respect to these writings there is one thing, however, about which we are not in doubt—namely, that these are truly *writings*. That is to say, they really are symbols that carry an encoded meaning. They are, therefore, intentional; they are contrived signs crafted by human hands at the service of human minds in order to communicate with other human minds. They *say* something, whatever it may be. They form what is called "text," and it is a distinguishing feature of human beings that they can discern such a thing as a text, even when they are unable to read it. Whatever doubts, questions, or conjectures may be raised with regard to the meaning of these texts, it would be irresponsible to suppose that, because we are unable to decipher them, these graphic marks are without intentional meaning. To suppose that they are not texts, not writings, would fly in the face of the massive countervailing evidence.

And exactly what is this evidence? Just how do we know that certain configurations on a clay tablet, or a series of markings on a rock or stick, or even a string of beads, forms a text, something to be *read*? How are we able to distinguish these lines and configurations from random scribbling or doodling? What is it about them that causes us to presume, and even insist, that they are intended to convey specific information?

Likewise, why do we not take them to be simply artistic embellishments of some sort, similar to symmetrical patterns that appear at far more distant periods of human history? Exactly what quality is it that prompts us to separate, as entirely new and special, the human markings that we find at Sumer and say, "Here is something truly different"?

Should we call that quality "intelligent design"? Well, perhaps, but I submit that this designation is really inadequate. After all, human beings produced very intelligent, highly crafted, graphic designs long before they began to write. And to this day we continue to produce mountains of intelligent designs that are not textual. Intelligent design does not necessarily convey information.

If we were asked to explain exactly how a written text differs from these other designs, we might even say that writing shows, in fact, a certain *lack* of design, in the sense of not being perfectly regular and symmetrical. Pieces of writing are marked by a sort of disparity, if you will, such as we would expect to find in a key, say, as distinct from a proportioned and uniform pattern.

To illustrate further: If I discover a sequence of graphic marks like /+0/+0/+0/+0 and so forth around the top of a vase, I am not likely to take this as an example of "text." Such a series of symbols is simply too regular to convey specific "information" of the sort I would expect in a spoken sentence, and I readily suspect that, while such marks demonstrate an intelligent design, that design pertains to the realm of decorative art rather than that of writing.

The latter contrivance, writing, though it certainly displays a structured form and consistency, is also characterized by a greater complexity, a subtle irregularity, and even a measure of unpredictability in its sequence; its various symbols do not fall into place with the serial recurrence of a perfectly metric pattern, but in certain periodic conjunctions, even elaborate configurations, appearing at intervals not dictated by concerns of symmetry. Most people know when they are looking at a piece of writing; they are able to distinguish it from both random scribbles on the one hand and purely esthetic designs on the other.

However, writing does have this quality in common with artistic design—that they are both recognized as "intentional," as distinct from random or haphazard. Both writings and artistic patterns are crafted with some defined purpose in mind, much as one would construct a tool. Indeed, this analogy with tools is worth considering. Ancient history has left us many examples of tools and implements whose distinct purpose we can only guess at. We look at certain ancient stone contrivances and can be perfectly sure that they were handheld implements designed for a specific purpose, while the purpose itself remains a mystery to us. That is to say, even though we are not sure of their purpose, we are nonetheless sure that they *had* a purpose, and this is how we recognize them as tools.

Such reflections demonstrate our ability to discern intelligibility even in things that remain unintelligible to us. We human beings can detect the presence of "mind" and the intent to convey "information" even in those instances when we are unable to decipher exactly what that information is or what that mind is trying to say. Human reason has an innate capacity, that is, for recognizing the presence of rationality. We are able to know when we are, in fact, dealing with a *text*.

In short, when we study the world, we find a text. The world *tells* us of God. Indeed, if it doesn't, we need not waste our time going to God's "second volume," which is Holy Scripture.

THE HEAVENS DECLARE

"The heavens declare the glory of God," wrote the psalmist, " . . . Day to day utters speech, / And night to night reveals knowledge. . . . Their proclamation went forth into all the earth, / And their words to the end of the world" (Psalm 18:1–5). The Apostle Paul would cite these very words, originally describing the message of Creation, as illustrating the universality of the apostolic preaching (Romans 10:18). And did not the psalmist also compare the final dissolution of the heavens to the rolling up of a scroll?

Armed with this biblical warrant, earlier Christians turned to the world with a distinctly *exegetical* interest. Examples of this interest are ubiquitous in Christian Latin literature. For instance, "These heavens," said St. Augustine, "these books, are the works of God's fingers," and St. Gregory the Great likened "the considered appearance of Creation" *(species considerata creaturae)* to "a sort of reading for our mind" *(quasi quaedam sit lectio menti nostrae)*. In the twelfth century, Alexander Neckam, the foster brother of Richard the Lionheart, remarked that "the world is inscribed with the pen of God; for anyone who understands it, it is a work of literature." Similarly and slightly earlier, Rupert of Deutz had commented that, as the Word Himself is "the architect of the world, he also . . . composed . . . Holy Scripture," and the Englishman, Herbert of Bosham, even called the work of Creation "a kind of corporeal and visible Gospel" *(velut quoddam evangelium corporale et visibile)*. Likewise, both Hugh and Richard of St. Victor wrote, "The whole of this sensible world is like a book written by the finger of God."

Perhaps no one spoke more often on this subject, however, than John Scotus Erigena in the ninth century. Commenting, for example, on the prologue of John's Gospel, he said that "the eternal light is proclaimed to the world in two ways, namely, Scripture and Creation." These form the double ladder of the divine ascent; commenting on the same Gospel, Erigena says later, "The first step in climbing the heights of virtue is the letter of Holy Scripture and the appearance of visible things, so that, once the letter has been read and creation examined, they may ascend, by the steps of correct reason, to the spirit of the letter and the rationality of creation." Erigena speaks of Creation and Holy Scripture as the two garments of Christ, a theme taken up three centuries later by Aelred of Rievaulx.

According to this traditional Christian view, the rationality of the universe, the clearly intentional disposition of its parts in relation to one another and to the whole, especially its relationship to man, is the sustaining subtext of the human narrative and the foundational context of poetry. This is why Holy Scripture begins with the account of Creation. It not only *happened* first; it is God's first "writing."

Within the traditions of the perennial philosophy and the Christian faith, there is no need for man to formulate human meaning fresh and out of whole cloth. He is expected to presume, as more or less obvious, that the universe is already possessed of a story line, that it is a rational and poetic place, in the sense of possessing a systematic coherence corresponding to the innate aspirations and essential structure of the human mind. The world and the intellect, in other words, were made for one another.

Moreover, according to this traditional Christian and classical view, it is this textual quality of the created world that justifies our going to it in pursuit of literary types. For a writer like Dante, for example, if the structure of the world already contains an elaborate message, a message both poetical and rational, Creation may itself be incorporated into man's literary endeavor as an active component. He finds in the world a pre-existing truth to be explored further by narrative. Beyond mere context, that is to say, Creation provides also the structural types that give coherence to storytelling. This conviction is part of the Christian birthright.

CREATION & THE TORAH

In one of those perceptive historical surveys that make his book so attractive, the son of Sirach meditates on the works of Creation, culminating in the human being, and continues with the gift of the Torah on Mount Sinai (Wisdom of Sirach 16:18—17:18).

Passing rather quickly through the first five days of Creation (16:25–30), Sirach looks more closely at the sixth day and the special gifts by which the Lord graced the existence of man (17:1–10). He recalls that the human being was made in God's image, which is expressed in his governance over other creatures. This dominion, in turn, is based on man's unique ability to think rationally, to reflect critically on his own act of thought, and to give creative narrative shape to the contents of his memory and imagination: "He put the fear of man upon all flesh / And gave him dominion over wild animals and birds. / He gave mankind the ability to deliberate, / And a tongue, eyes and ears, and a heart to think with" (17:4–5).

This construction of man's being was, in fact, God's first revelation to man's reflective mind, whereby he was endowed with an innate moral sense: "He filled them with the skill of comprehension / And showed them good and evil. . . . He added knowledge to them / And gave them the law of life as a heritage" (17:6, 9).

This revelation included also a rational impulse to regard Creation as the disclosure of divine truth and glory: "He set His eye upon their hearts / To show them the majesty of His works. / They will praise His holy name / So as to fully describe the majesty of His works" (17:7–8).

To say that God set His eye on the human heart is to proclaim the deepest truth of man as a moral being. So, when a man truly discovers his heart, he uncovers it as something already known and accounted for by Someone Else. This is so true, indeed, that a man does not truly *find* his heart except as the object of the divine scrutiny. That is to say, man knows God through the personal discovery that God knows him. I suggest, moreover, that this sense of standing under the divine gaze is the precondition of faith, which is the primal, necessary channel of man's communion with God.

Thus, before going on to speak of God's historical revelation on Mount Sinai, Sirach feels obliged to reflect on an essential condition that makes human history possible. Man's history, after all, is not just another dimension of "natural history," because the human being represents a radical discontinuity from all other creatures. This discontinuity is found in God's endowment of the human soul with the specific capacity for history. Other things exist through the passage of time, but they don't really have a history. Strictly speaking, it is only the human being that can have a history, because only the human being is qualified to reflect critically on the events that take place in time and to arrange those events in narrative form.

Thus, and more specifically, Sirach cannot speak of God's Self-revelation in history until he establishes that principle, innate in man, by which God's historical revelation can be recognized. That is to say, what God does in history cannot be known as revelation unless God first confers on the human heart an impulse toward narrative, a capacity to recall—to call back—in story form, an innate disposition to review the human experience in a structured account. In other words, there can be such a thing as human history because God first placed in the human soul the impulse towards historiography. Man can have a history only because God created him as a storyteller.

This native impulse toward historiography, however, which is distinctively human, is a moral instinct. Storytelling is essentially an artistic effort to confer shape on the soul.

And this, in turn, is essential to historical revelation. If history cannot carry human meaning, then history certainly cannot bear the immense burden of divine revelation.

Such is the continuity that Sirach perceives between the creation of man in Genesis and the gift of the Torah in Exodus. There is a narrative continuity between the two because they form one metaphysical and moral extension, a single divine revelation, in both nature and history.

In short, there would be no point in the Bible's recording every word that proceeded from the mouth of God unless there already existed in the world that rational, moral, storytelling creature that finds himself unable to live by bread alone.

THE METAPHYSICS OF MOSES

Not so terribly long ago, the normal college survey course in the history of philosophy began with the pre-Socratics, went on to the classical period of Plato and Aristotle, maybe noticed the Stoics and the Neoplatonists, moved into early Christian philosophy (often enough reduced to St. Augustine), proceeded to the medieval Schoolmen, and came finally to the modern period. This last period, beginning roughly with Bacon and Hobbes, I suppose, took up about half of the textbook.

Nowadays, however, when I have occasion to speak to college students, I learn that many contemporary survey courses on the history of philosophy do not include anybody between Plotinus (AD third century) and Descartes (first half of the seventeenth century). That is to say, more than a millennium of Western thought is simply eliminated. I live within walking distance of a university where this is the case.

Obviously this new arrangement is designed to preserve the discipline of philosophy from "contamination" by "revealed religion," specifically the Bible. That is to say, there is no room for Moses. Christians may not be disposed to complain about this, because we are not accustomed to thinking about Moses as a philosopher. Correctly so.

On the other hand, there is simply no understanding the history of Western philosophy if we leave Moses out of the picture. The disadvantage of doing so can be measured in two respects, I believe, both of them historical.

First, this new approach to the history of philosophy, leaving out everything revealed in the Bible, fails by the most elementary criterion of history. No historical study of any subject can simply skip a thousand years at will. Imagine a history of weapons that leaped over everything from the slingshot to intercontinental ballistic missiles. Suppose the writer of such a study argued, in defense of this method, that he didn't want his study of weapons to be "contaminated" by considerations of the sword or the introduction of saltpeter. Sound likely?

Neither is it feasible for some person's biographer to decide he will skip ages 20 to 45 of that person's life. Suppose Gerald Clarke, for instance, in his biography of Truman Capote, had written about Capote's childhood up to about age 19 and then skipped the rest of his life up to the final ten years. We would scarcely know that Capote is mainly remembered as a writer. Would anyone agree that this was a useful biography? The idea is just as silly in the history of philosophy as it is in the life of Capote.

History, after all, has to do with continuity, so a "history of philosophy" is not really a history if it is not continuous. You can't skip the middle thousand years of 2500 years of history. And that middle millennium was dominated by what Gilson called "the metaphysics of Moses."

The second disadvantage also pertains to history, and it is this. During the "skipped" period in question, the era of Christian philosophy, it is arguable that philosophy itself was more directly tied to the formation of popular culture than at any other period of man's time on this earth.

After all, the average man on the street in classical Athens did not think along lines in the least like Plato (a fact Plato knew very well and sometimes grumbled about). Again, precious few people in the seventeenth century thought along lines like those of Descartes or Spinoza (for which circumstance may a merciful Providence be praised). During both its very early and very recent periods, that is to say, philosophy was largely the domain of the intellectual elites, not the common property of ordinary people.

The very opposite was true during the period of Christian philosophy. Whatever else we may say about the metaphysics of Moses, it did provide a truly popular philosophy. For a millennium and a half, every Christian in the world knew the basics of Christian philosophy. If we ask what these basics were—which were the most characteristic and most significant ideas the Christian Church added to the history of philosophy—the first two answers would have to be (if my shorthand is permitted) "Being" and "beings." Christians learned about "Being" from Exodus 3 ("I Am Who Am"), and about "beings" from Genesis 1 ("In the beginning God created the heavens and the earth").

First, Being. According to Christian philosophy, God is the eternal, personal, and necessary Being (He who, if He does exist, must exist). The God "whose being is to be" never entered the mind of classical philosophy. Neither Plato nor Aristotle identified God in these terms. Christian philosophy, however, "contaminated" by the Bible, derived this concept from Exodus 3:14—*ego eimi ho on*— "I Am He Who Is." The simplest Christian, the believer least given to philosophical speculation, knew this. No elite education was required. This concept formed the basis of a whole new culture that utterly transformed the history of all who received the Christian Gospel.

Second, beings. According to Christian philosophy, learned at the feet of Moses, God created from nothingness all other things that are. No thing, outside of God, has its existence except by God's creating act. Classical pagan philosophy never dreamed of such a thing. Once again, however, Christian philosophy, still hopelessly "corrupted" by Holy Writ, knew this from the opening of Genesis: "In the beginning God made heaven and earth." No advanced study was necessary to grasp this idea. The least educated Christian knew it.

As soon as folks heard these two ideas for the first time, they suddenly thought to themselves, "Well, obviously. Now that you say it, Moses, it's as clear as day. The ideas are perfectly coherent and compelling. Darn, I wonder why we never thought of it before" (I paraphrase St. Augustine, *Confessions* 11.3.5). These ideas, perfectly self-evident on being enunciated, were the foundation stones of Christian philosophy.

In the early second century Hermas of Rome laid out the case succinctly: "Before all else believe that there exists only one God, who created and finished all things, and brought all things into being out of nothing" (*The Shepherd*, Mandata 1.1).

FROM SALVATION TO CREATION

If one looks for the "assured results" of modern biblical studies (and, frankly, I think they are few), one of them seems to be a greater awareness that the theologians who wrote Holy Scripture began with the revelatory events of history, not the contemplation of nature. That is to say, the human authors of Holy Scripture approached Creation itself through the path of salvation history. They arrived at the knowledge of the Creator through their knowledge of the Lord of history. It was Exodus that led them to Genesis! In the words of a modern scholar of the Bible, Israel went "from the God who saves to the God who creates" (*du Dieu qui sauve au Dieu qui crée*—Trophime Mouiren).

This historical progress of biblical revelation does not mean, surely, that God cannot be known through the study of created things. Indeed, Holy Scripture asserts exactly the opposite, declaring that God's "invisible *attributes* are clearly seen, being understood by the things that are made, *even* His eternal power and Godhead" (Romans 1:20; cf. Wisdom of Solomon 13:1–7). Moreover, this "natural" revelation of God in His created works is very much a presumption of biblical apologetics (cf. Isaiah 42:5; Acts 17:22–24).

The essentially historical nature of divine revelation means, rather, that the biblical writers, even when they considered God as Creator, always identified that Creator as the Lord whom they first knew through His free and marvelous deeds of deliverance and covenant. It was the God of the holy ark who created all things, declared Hezekiah (Isaiah 37:16; 2 Kings 19:15). It was the "Redeemer" that gave form to the child in the womb (Isaiah 44:24).

The Bible's understanding of history is the key, therefore, to its understanding of Creation. Just as the Lord's activity in history is free, redemptive, and covenantal, so is His act of creating. For this reason, biblical reflection on God's created world regards Creation itself as the medium of salvation and covenant. The Bible, consequently, resists all effort to let Creation "stand on its own." It never looks at the created world through the lens of a philosophical abstraction that dehistoricizes the particular into the general. Revelation never declines into mere philosophy. Creation is as much a unique, singular event as the parting of the Red Sea or the call of Jeremiah. Moses refuses to succumb to Aristotelianism. The

Bible's view of Creation is as innocent of causal determinism as its view of history.

Perhaps we may let Ben Sirach illustrate the point. "The sun gives light and looks down on everything," he wrote, "And its work is full of the Lord's glory. / The Lord did not enable His saints / To describe all His wonders, / Which the Lord Almighty established / That the universe might be established in His glory" (Wisdom of Sirach 42:16–17). God's glory, that is to say, is not revealed through man's abstract theories about Creation, but through the individual, concrete, created things themselves. Their very incomprehensibility, moreover, is revelatory. Indeed, says Sirach, even the saints are unable to recount all God's marvelous works.

Among those who have commented on this biblical passage over the centuries, I wonder if any demonstrated more insight than Thomas Aquinas, who invoked this text in Sirach to illustrate the difference between biblical faith and philosophical discipline. Both faith and philosophy cast their regard on the created world, St. Thomas admits, but they do so very differently. The philosopher looks at a created thing according to its generic and formal qualities (*secundum quod huiusmodi*), whereas the Christian faith looks at it, not in this abstract way, but rather "inasmuch as it represents the divine depth [*divinam altitudinem*] and is in some way ordered toward God Himself [*in ipsum Deum quoquo modo ordinatur*]."

Like the historical progression of the Bible, which goes from history to the created world, the "believer" (*fidelis*) starts with God revealed in history, not with the study of the created world. This distinction is what separates the believer from the philosopher. The latter seeks the intrinsic causes of things (*ex propriis rerum causis*) in order to understand them, because understanding is the knowledge of things in their causes. The believer, on the contrary, starts with and proceeds from the First Cause in order to perceive created things as "divinely given, or as pertaining to the divine glory." The philosopher commences with the world that surrounds him, and he endeavors to grasp these things in their proper natures. The believer, however, begins with the historically revealed Lord, whose creative act, manifesting His glory, holds these things in existence (*Summa Contra Gentiles* 2.4).

I believe St. Thomas shows great insight here. If reflection on

Creation is to be properly theological, it must begin with the God who reveals Himself in history through His deeds of deliverance and covenant. Deliverance and covenant must also confer shape on the lens for the Christian study of the created world. Otherwise *de Deo creante* will diminish into mere cosmology . . . or worse. It may degenerate into the alleged objectivity and autonomy arbitrarily and imperiously demanded by the contemporary sciences. In contrast to all this, God's free and redemptive intervention in history opens the door to the orthodox understanding of His Creation.

CREATION AND CHRISTOLOGY

Among the doctrines of the New Testament most neglected these days, I submit, is that of Christ as Mediator. Well, perhaps "neglected" is too strong. Let's say, "severely reduced."

An indication of this reduction, I believe, is the widespread failure of contemporary Christians to mention or even to think of the mediation of Christ when they speak of Creation, either of its structure or of our understanding of that structure. In other words, I believe that Christians nowadays rarely regard Christ with respect to cosmology and epistemology. Since, however, we are to love God with our "whole mind," it is surely not legitimate to remove Christ from either concern. To reflect on the Christology of Creation, therefore, we will consider both cosmology and epistemology.

First, cosmology. Cosmology addresses the question, "How are things put together?" And the Christian answers, "Things are put together in Christ. In Him all things subsist." Several places in the New Testament provide starting points for a Christocentric cosmology, I suppose, but 2 Corinthians 4:6 will do as well as any: "For it is the God who commanded light to shine out of darkness, who has shone in our hearts to give the light of the knowledge of the glory of God in the face of Jesus Christ." In this text, we observe that Paul identifies the Creator in Genesis as the same God whose light shines out from the face of Christ.

Now it is Paul's thesis that this very light of Creation is disclosed on the face of Christ. He contends that it is through Christ that the mysterious, otherwise invisible light of Creation is rendered manifest. The knowledge of God in Christ reveals this light "in our hearts."

This, I submit, is one of the very important but often neglected senses in which Christ is the Mediator. It was with reference to Christ, too, that St. John asserted, in his own treatment on cosmology, "He was in the beginning with God. All things were made through Him" (John 1:2–3). John, then, agrees with Moses about the light in Creation. Accordingly, we should begin with Jesus, "the One from whom the two greatest Wise Men began: Moses the originator of Wisdom, and John, its consummator" (St. Bonaventure, *In Hexaemeron* 1.10).

In sum, according to the theology of Paul and John, Christ is our Mediator even in the sense of the world's formal composition. In addition to the uncreated light that emanates from His divine Person, there shines also the created light that gives structure and essence to the universe.

And this thesis brings us to the epistemological question, "How can I *know* this meaning at the heart of Creation?" Paul and John address this question as well. For them, Christ is not only the mediator *of* Creation, the Word in whom all created things subsist and have their being; He is also the intelligible light by which His own mediation is perceived. That is, Christ is not only the cosmological foundation of all created things but also the epistemological principle, through whom all things created are known to God and may, in divine revelation, be understood by men. Coming into the world, says John, He enlightened every man (John 1:9).

For this reason, it is the thesis of the Bible that the true and ultimate intelligibility of the world is concealed from those who do not know Christ. On this point, let us stay with St. Paul, who prays that we may "[*attain*] to all riches of the full assurance of understanding, to the knowledge of the mystery of God, both of the Father and of Christ, in whom are hidden all the treasures of wisdom and knowledge" (Colossians 2:3).

Observe that in Christ the treasures of wisdom and knowledge are said to be "hidden"—*apokryphoi*. Jesus too spoke of this concealment: "I thank You, Father, Lord of heaven and earth, that You have hidden [*ekrypsas*] these things from *the* wise and prudent and have revealed them to babes" (Matthew 11:25). God's *Logos* within the world is first a work of cryptography and then of disclosure.

The lens of Christ, then, provides the "correct vision"—the "orthodoxy"—of the world, including its origin out of nothingness and its final transformation unto immortality. The meaning of all things created is concealed in the Person and life of Jesus and revealed to the little ones that entrust themselves to His sole mediation. Christ is the focus of the metaphysics of Moses: "For if you believed Moses, you would believe Me; for he wrote about Me" (John 5:46).

The structural principle and the final destiny of Creation, then, are manifest at a specific point in history, which point is known by the name Jesus Christ. Ultimately, no view of the world is really correct, truly orthodox, except through the lightsome lens of faith in the mediation of the Man Jesus Christ.

PART ONE
CREATION AND PRIMEVAL HISTORY

～ GENESIS 1 ～

The opening chapter of Genesis has long been a favorite of Christians, and ancient commentators discovered in its lines profound levels of meaning. In more recent times, on the other hand, some readers of Genesis, distracted by apologetic concerns alien to the deeper interests of the Sacred Text, have failed to discover those depths. For example, even from boyhood I recall that some of my teachers were preoccupied with the length of the six "days" of Creation. Was it really necessary, they asked, to think of those "days" in the sense of having twenty-four hours? Might they not, instead, represent long periods of natural history?

The problem with such questions is that they distract the mind from the deeper message of the Sacred Text. It is safe to say that the Bible nowhere thinks of a day in our modern sense of the time required for a complete revolution of the earth. A biblical "day" is normally a *standard* of measurement, not an object to be measured. Nearly from the beginning, therefore, Christians have been reluctant to measure the length of the days of Creation. This reluctance was perhaps summarized by St. Augustine of Hippo about the year 416: "What sort of days these were, it is very difficult or perhaps impossible for us to conceive, and how much more to say!" (*The City of God* 11.6).

Moreover, several ancient Christian readers of Genesis observed what seems to have escaped the notice of some modern readers—namely, that the sun was not created until the fourth day. There were three days of light and darkness before there was a sun to rise or set.

Indeed, this observation is partly the point. The setting and rising of the sun are not what determine day and night. We moderns think of the sunlight as that which creates the day, and the absence of sunlight as that which creates night. There is nothing of that idea here in Genesis. The Bible and its ancient commentators would have thought this a very shallow notion of day and night, light and darkness. In biblical thought, the sun "marks" the day; it does not create it. The day would be here, so to speak, whether the sun rose or not. The purpose of the sun is to enable us to see that it *is* day. Evening and morning, however, already existed for three days before there ever *was* a sun.

Day and night are simply the names of light and darkness (v. 5); light and darkness exist independent of the sun or any other heavenly body. We note that Genesis does not say that God creates darkness; darkness was, so to speak, already there. Darkness is nothingness; it is nonexistence. Therefore night itself is symbolic of nonexistence. This is why night will eventually disappear (Revelation 22:5).

Light, on the other hand, is the first creation of God; "Let there be light" are His first recorded words (v. 3). The light, then, and the darkness, which are called day and night, refer to something far deeper in Creation than the phenomena that our eyes behold. Light is not simply a byproduct of solar energy. It is, rather, the principle of intelligibility in the structure of Creation. The light that God calls into being at the beginning of Genesis is that inner structure of intelligibility that the mind of man, in due course, will be created to discover and investigate. Man's investigation of the light is called philosophy, just as his investigation of God's Word is called theology.

In the biblical narrative of the Creation, it is noteworthy that the original day of Creation is not designated "the first" day. It is called, rather, "one day" (*yom 'ehad*). Although this difference of expression in verse 5 has proved too subtle for virtually all biblical translations into modern languages (the *Orthodox Study Bible* being a happy exception!), its significance caused it to be maintained in the ancient versions, such as the Septuagint (*hemera mia*) and the Vulgate (*dies unus*). In addition, that difference of expression ("one day" instead of "first day") was the object of explicit discussion in nearly all ancient commentaries on verse 5, whether Jewish (e.g., Philo and Rashi) or Christian (e.g., Basil and Augustine). Alas, the difference seems excessively subtle to modern minds, which come to the first chapter of Genesis as though it were a text of astrophysics.

In those ancient and classical commentaries on this biblical text, moreover, we find the common assertion that the words "one day" served to elevate that day of Creation to something more than part of a sequence. There is a profound reason why the original day of Creation is appropriately called "one," whereas the second day is not appropriately called "two," nor the third day "three," and so forth. The original day is "one" in a manner analogous to the number itself. "One" is not simply the numeral that precedes two; it is, rather, the number out of which that second number comes. There is a formal disparity between one and the other numbers. One (*to hen*) is the font determining the identity of two and the subsequent numbers. "One" is not just "first" as part of a sequence; it is what we call a principle, an *arche*. On "day one," then, God creates light, which He thereby separates from darkness. It is out of this light, which is the product of God's first creating word, that all the rest of Creation comes. All things that God makes are filled with His light. God's light lies shining at the heart of the world.

Excursus:
Creation *Ex Nihilo*

In our regular recitation of the Creed that binds us together, we first declare our faith "in one God, the Father almighty, the Maker of heaven and earth, and of all things, visible and invisible." The Church has always understood this declaration to refer to two aspects of God, God in eternity and God in time. From all eternity He is the Father; in the realm of time He is the Creator. It is this second aspect that I want to consider now. What does it mean that God is the Creator of "heaven and earth, and of all things visible and invisible"? There are three points to be considered on this subject.

We should reflect, first, that this is a revealed truth. Creation refers to a specific act that cannot be reached by the power of reason. Creation, as the Christian faith understands that term, means the passage from non-being to being. I do not know, nor can I know, by the ability of reason, that all things, visible and invisible, have passed from non-being to being.

My reason tells me, of course, that I myself and the world around me have a rational source. The intelligent design that my reason beholds in the universe cannot possibly have come from a series of undirected accidents; my mind cries out that it is utterly irrational to imagine otherwise. Only a fool would affirm it. (In fact, the Bible uses the word "fool" when it mentions this possibility.)

Still, the intelligent design I see in the world does not tell me that all things, visible and invisible, come from nothing. Science and philosophy have never breathed a word of it. Creation is a truth divinely revealed, which is why it is contained in the Creed. It is not the business of the Creed, after all, to affirm things that can be affirmed apart from the Creed.

How, then, do I know that all things have been created from nothing? To borrow a phrase, "this I know for the Bible tells me so." Typical of the Christian conviction on this point, one may cite St. Hilary of Poitiers: "For all things, as the prophet says, were made out of nothing; it was no transformation of existing things, but the creation of non-being into a perfect form" (De Trinitate 4.16).

Who was this "prophet" cited by St. Hilary? In fact, it was a prophetess, because St. Hilary was quoting the mother of the Maccabean martyrs, who said to one of her tortured sons, "I beseech you, my child, to look at heaven and earth and see everything in them, and know that God made them out of nothing; so also He made the race of man in this way" (2 Maccabees 7:28). This text from 2 Maccabees was the standard biblical proof text for the Christian

Church in respect to creation from nothingness. We find the thesis in late Judaism, from which it passed into the Christian faith as an essential teaching.

But it is important to reflect that we believe it as revealed by God, and we have no access to that truth except through divine revelation. Creation is an absolutely unique act of the biblical God. Philosophy and science know nothing of it. This is why there can be no such thing as "creation science."

Second, what has been created from nothing? We affirm, "heaven and earth, and all things visible and invisible." Not just earth, we understand, but heaven too. Not just the material world that we see, but also the invisible world that we cannot see. Not just the chemical substances of things, but also the mathematical theorems and physical laws that give them coherence. Everything that is not God has been created from nothingness, no matter how high, how metaphysical, how spiritual. Apart from God, there is absolutely nothing that was not made from nothing.

No part of Creation, then, is an emanation of the divine being. Nothing of God's essence has passed into what He has made. Not only is the human brain created from nothing, but also the spiritual human intellect that uses that brain; and not only the human intellect but also the rational principles by which that intellect functions. The very laws of logic have been created from nothing. According to a summary of St. Bonaventure, "The world was produced in being, and not only according to itself as a whole, but also according to its intrinsic principles [sed etiam secundum sua intrinseca principia], which were not produced from other things but from nothing" (On the Sentences 2.1.1.1).

Third, God's creating act is the only thing that separates all things from nothing. No creature is adequately considered, then, if it is considered only *in se*, in itself. Creatures do not have their being *a se*, of themselves. They are held in existence only because an immense and continuing act of love holds them in existence. All things that endure, endure because the Creator's hand sustains them in being.

Each of us is held in existence by this same act of unspeakable love. We depend utterly on the sustained activity of the Creator, in whom we live and move and have our being. Even when I disobey God and stray from Him, God holds me in existence. Even when I insult Him and spit in His face, God's creating love preserves me in being. His hands ever fashion me and sustain me.

Under this consideration, who is the wise man? The wise man is the one who knows this truth and lives on the basis of it. He does not pretend that he has an independent existence, which is a mirage and a deception. If the doctrine of Creation is true, the wise man is the one who finds that place in his being where God touches him and holds him in existence. The wise man does not pretend that he is anything *in se*, in himself. His very existence is a created existence, and the Holy Scriptures give him the wisdom to know this.

This, then, is the first declaration contained in our Creed, and it is a declaration of dependence. This is the wisdom handed down in the Holy Scriptures and affirmed in our faith.

❧ GENESIS 2 ❧

To even the simplest reader of the Bible it is obvious that there are two accounts of Creation in the first two chapters of Genesis. Both of them are theological interpretations of the *fact* of Creation; more to the point, they are *different* theological interpretations, analogous to the differences we find among the four canonical Gospels.

Chapter 1 deals with Creation from nothingness; that is to say, there is no pre-existent matter out of which God creates. The Hebrew word used to designate this Creation is *barah*. By spreading Creation over six days, followed by the Sabbath rest, the inspired author structures the Jewish week into the structure of time itself. He views man as the final product and pinnacle of Creation.

In this second account of Creation everything takes place much faster. Although man is said to sleep, night is never mentioned. Here God is said to "form" (*yasar*), to give shape to; it is the word normally used for working in ceramics. Indeed, man is shaped from the moist soil, the mud, like the work of pottery to which Jeremiah will later compare him. In this chapter of Genesis the plants and animals are not created until *after* the creation of man. Man is created in order to take care of the plants (vv. 7–15), while the animals are created to be man's companions (vv. 18–20). The very word for "man" is the Hebrew generic word for a human being, *adam*, related to the *adamah*, or the "soil" from which he comes.

Still, this first human being is a male. Therefore, the noun designating him is masculine in gender. (The word for "human being" in all languages, by the way, is unvaryingly masculine; for example, *ha'adam* in Hebrew, *ho anthropos* in Greek, *'nôshô'* in Syriac, *al-insan* in Arabic, *chelovyek* in Russian, *der Mensch* in German, *de man* in Dutch, *zmogùs* in Lithuanian, *njerí* in Albanian, *man* in English, *homo* in Latin, along with its multiple derivatives in Italian, Spanish, Portuguese, Romanian, French, and even English (such as the adjective "human"). And so forth. In their respective languages, all these nouns are *masculine* in gender.) Contrary to the contemporary conceit that pretends otherwise, there is no such thing as a non-gendered, gender-neutral noun for a human being. While the sex of an actual human being is either male or female, the gender of the designating noun is invariably masculine. This distinction, alas, tends to be lost on those who, having confused grammar with biology, go on to confuse gender with sex.

It is from this first man, Adam, that the first woman is formed. More specifically, it is from the part of man closest to his heart, from the place where woman herself lives, at man's side. But she comes from within him; when Adam sees her, he recognizes this "bone of my bone and flesh of my flesh." She is, as it were, part of him. The sexual attraction between men and women, in the eyes of the Bible, is metaphysical, having to do with an essential craving for inner wholeness (v. 24). Jesus will later on appeal to this truth as the basis for His prohibition of divorce (Mark 10:8–9; 1 Corinthians 6:16–17; Ephesians 5:31–32). It also serves as the biblical argument against sexual activity outside of the marriage between a man and a woman. Any sexual activity that does not involve one man and one woman, married to one another, stands outside of the proper moral structure of human sexuality itself. This is one of the major applications of man's transcendence of the animals.

Excursus:
Faith and Natural Revelation

There are two apparently irreconcilable aspects to the New Testament's affirmation of natural revelation—the knowledge of God available in the data of the created world.

On the one hand, it is affirmed that man is able to discover God's existence from examining His works in nature, because "since the creation of the world His invisible attributes are clearly seen, being understood by the things that are made, even His eternal power and Godhead" (Romans 1:20). There is not a word in this text about faith. Indeed, how can one *believe* in what is "clearly seen"?

On the other hand, it is equally attested that "he who comes to God must *believe* that He is" (Hebrews 11:6). Faith, not reason, is affirmed here. However, if faith in God's existence is necessary, how am I to have faith in what I already know? How is it possible to know and believe in the same thing?

I did not make up this problem. The mutual exclusivity of faith and reason, when both are directed to the same object and under the same aspect, has always been recognized among rational men as a rational problem. Hugh of St. Victor was hardly alone when he asserted, "Those things that are entirely known by reason [ex ratione omnino nota sunt] cannot be believed, because they are known" (De Sacramentis 1.3.20). That is to say, no faith is necessary, or even possible, in propositions demonstrated by reason. If, then, I already know God's existence by reason (as I most certainly do), how is it possible for me to believe it? And yet, if I do not believe in it, how can I come to God, as the Epistle to the Hebrews says?

Since both things are affirmed in Holy Scripture, however, one suspects what we have here is a mystery, not a just a philosophical dilemma, and I want to suggest two avenues to the consideration of this mystery.

The first avenue, elaborated by St. Bonaventure, concentrates on the special sense of "knowing" when this verb refers to God as an object. When a thinker arrives at the inference "God" at the end of a logical argument, he does not know God as he knows some other object of his rational regard. He does not perceive God as he perceives, for instance, the principle of non-contradiction, or the theorems of mathematics, or the validity of the Baroco syllogism. God does not give form to his intellect in the same way that his intellect is informed by rational truths. God remains God and therefore inaccessible to the mind's comprehension.

Bonaventure writes, "Someone who believes that God is one and is the Creator of all, if he should begin to know this same fact [ipsum idem] from arguments of rational necessity, does not for this reason stop believing; likewise, if someone should already know this, the arrival of faith does not remove the knowledge of it. Our experience testifies to this."

With regard to reason's knowledge of God's existence, Bonaventure says, "The light and certitude of this knowledge is not such that, having it, the light of faith is superfluous; indeed, it is necessary with it." Therefore, he concludes that, in the case of God, knowing and believing "are compatible, simultaneously and in the same respect" (*On the Sentences* 3.24.2,3).

The Seraphic Doctor's approach to this question prompts a second one of my own. I begin with "contingent being"—those things that exist but do not have to exist (which is to say, everything created, everything except God). When I argue from the existence of contingent beings to the existence of Necessary Being (which I have always considered the most compelling and irreducible of the cosmological arguments, bolstered by its application in Wisdom of Solomon 13 and Romans 1), I do not arrive simply at an abstract rational truth, but at a Being on whom all other things, including myself, are *contingent*. The prefix of this word is the key. I arrive at a Being by whom all things else are touched (*con-tingo*).

This may be a purely rational process, but only until the moment I reach the inference of my argument, because the Being I reach, the Being on whom all other things depend, is necessarily a Being of knowledge and volition, revealed in the very act of causing created things to be. For contingent being (created things) to exist, after all, it is obvious that some will or decision is required of the Necessary Being. Therefore, the Necessary Being must be personal, in a sense analogous to ourselves as persons, a Being who knows and wills. This is not the Prime Mover of Aristotle, but the God who identified Himself to Moses from the burning bush as "He Who Is," the One in whom to be is *necessarily* to be, the One that cannot be thought of as not existing.

I cannot relate to such a Being simply as a concept in my mind (which it most certainly is *not*). My mind itself screams out against such a presumption,

for to know God in this way is to be *known by* God.
To know God as the source of my being is to know
Him at that point where He maintains me in being.
As a matter of experience, then, it is impossible for
me to separate *scio Deum* from *credo Deo*. That is
to say, I am unable to affirm that God exists without
recognizing and confessing my dependence on Him,
and fixing my mind in that dependence. Contin-
gency here implies dependency. In the rational act
of arriving at His existence ("I Am Who Am") I am
drawn toward God as a personal Reality, the real
God who knows me and wills me. I cannot help
recognizing my utter dependence on Him, and the
rational recognition of this dependence is faith: "But
without faith *it is* impossible to please *Him*, for he
who comes to God must believe that He is, and *that*
He is a rewarder of those who diligently seek Him"
(Hebrews 11:6).

ᔑ GENESIS 3 ᔐ

Probably because she was the world's first offender, Holy Scripture
goes into some detail to describe the temptation to which Eve succumbed. Her temptation serving as a kind of paradigm of all temptation, Eve stands as the Bible's first negative model of the moral life;
her lapse provides the initial description of how the demons deal
with the human soul.

Perhaps, indeed, St. Paul was indicating as much when he wrote
to the church at Corinth, "I fear, lest somehow, as the serpent deceived Eve by his craftiness, so your minds may be corrupted from the
simplicity that is in Christ" (2 Corinthians 11:3). Thus, if we want
to understand how temptation functions in human psychology, we
can hardly do better than to examine the temptation of Eve.

Prior to succumbing, Eve is tempted in three stages: (1) "So when
the woman saw the tree was good for food," (2) "was pleasant to the
eyes," (3) "and a tree desirable to make one wise" (NKJV)—"she took

its fruit and ate" (v. 6). We may reasonably say that these three steps in the temptation correspond to "all that *is* in the world"—namely, "the lust of the flesh ['good for food'], the lust of the eyes ['pleasant to the eyes'], and the pride of life ['desirable to make one wise']" (1 John 2:16). At each stage in the temptation, Eve indulges a specious reasoning begotten of her passions. Objective moral strictures are not consulted. Eve's Fall results from a distorted pattern of reasoning, for her thoughts are dictated by her desires.

And how did Eve stumble into this tripartite temptation? By giving ear to the deceptive arguments of the serpent. The latter begins with a factual question: "Has God indeed said, 'You shall not eat from every tree of the garden'?" (v. 1). The idea is preposterous, and Eve hastens to correct the questioner. She feels justified in this, of course, because in answering the serpent she can even feel herself to be God's defender. Alas, however, a conversation with the deceiver has therewith begun, and fickle Eve is a poor match for him. Her first mistake, then, was tactical. She should never have answered him at all.

Eve's mind now engaged, the deceiver prompts her to question the very reason God had given for the command, "for in whatever day you eat from it, you shall die by death" (2:17). In fact, Eve had never heard God say these words, for they were spoken before she was formed from Adam's rib. Eve knew of the prohibition only through Adam. That is to say, God's mandate, as far as Eve knew, was simply a moral tradition, perhaps subject to improvement. Why need she submit her moral judgment to the apodictic command that Adam had shared with her? She, after all, had a mind of her own. She was just as intelligent as Adam, who after all had not really been in this world much longer than she. She could figure things out for herself. Thus did our ancient mother commence the process of her own personal moral theory.

St. Paul describes Eve's beguilement as a corruption from "simplicity" (2 Corinthians 11:3). In place of God's emphatic command, known solely through the moral tradition available to her, Eve declared the autonomy of her own thought, not pausing to consider that her thinking was hardly more than the perverse assertion of her passions.

We notice several effects of the Fall. First, Adam and Eve become aware of themselves as naked, as exposed. They are no longer comfortable with themselves (v. 7). They hide from God (v. 8). Then, when God questions Adam, the latter immediately casts the blame on his wife, and indirectly on God Himself, who gave Adam that wife (vv. 11–12). Eve in her turn blames the snake (v. 12). God then curses all three, in reverse order: first the snake (vv. 14–15), then Eve (v. 16), and finally Adam (vv. 17–19).

Even as God drives Adam and Eve from the garden, however, He provides better clothing for them (v. 21). This is important. Man's sin created the problem of nakedness, and hence the solution of clothing, as described here in chapter 3. In the Bible's final book, nonetheless, when man's sin has in every last sense been conquered, we do not see the human race returned to the nakedness of its primitive, unfallen state. The new man in Christ is clothed. We are described in the Book of Revelation as wearing the white robes of glory. Grace, that is to say, does more than reverse the effects of sin; it transforms the effects of sin. Our new innocence in Christ is not to be identified as simply the earlier innocence of Adam. The effect of sin is not merely removed; it is assumed into a more ample transformation.

As we go on in Genesis and the rest of Holy Scripture, we will meet other examples of this mysterious transformation of certain human experiences, especially cultural forms, that are associated in their origin, or at least their earliest historical expression, with the Fall. That is to say, the new life in Christ includes His taking hold of and entirely remolding certain components of life that were not part of man's original, innocent state. Even as He vanquishes sin, God does not simply undo or reverse the effects of man's Fall. Rather, He assumes these same effects, particularly cultural effects, into a larger expression of man's ascent.

The human race has fallen in chapter 3. Man is about to fall even lower in chapter 4.

Excursus:
Lost and Cursed

When we think of Adam's Fall, there are two passive participles that should come forcefully to our minds: *lost* and *cursed*. These two words sum up the human condition without Christ.

First, man is lost. Worse, he continues to get lost. It is a mistake to think of the fallen human being as somehow looking for God. Indeed, the very opposite is true. When the human race fell in Adam, a kind of spiritual inertia came into play, a force that kept him going in the same direction—away from God. Of himself man had no power of initiative to reverse the movement. This is what is meant by the Fall.

If man was to return to God, God had to take the initiative. If God had not sought man out, he would have kept going in the same direction—away. This is very clear in the biblical story of Adam's hiding from God immediately after his disobedience. He and all his descendants would still be lying low there in the bushes if God had not come after him, inquiring, "Where are you?"

It was not that God did not know where to find Adam. It was Adam who was lost, not God. God knew where Adam was, but Adam didn't. God's query, "Where are you?" was intended to wake lost man up to his real situation. As such, it was the first proclamation of the Gospel, the merciful word that began to reverse the direction of man's existence. Indeed, it was the first step toward the mystery of the Incarnation.

This divine inquiry was necessary because man had no interest in finding God. It was of God, on the contrary, that Adam was most afraid, because God recognized him to be naked. God understood this and promptly provided a covering for man's nakedness. It was the initial step toward man's final clothing, indicated in St. Paul's exhortation to "put on the Lord Jesus Christ" (Romans 13:14).

But even when confronted by his sin, Adam did not accept the accompanying guilt and responsibility. He immediately blamed Eve: "The woman You gave me, gave me of the tree, and I ate" (3:12). Indeed, this response even seems to blame God for the Fall. Adam speaks of Eve as "the woman You gave me," as though to say, "I did not ask for a wife; this whole arrangement was Your idea. This woman, whom You designed, is the one who got me into this mess."

Eve, for her part, follows Adam's example of passing the blame: "The serpent deceived me, and I ate" (3:13). This too was God's fault, of course, because He created this "creeping thing" (1:25). Eve could hardly hold herself responsible for what had happened.

Even found, that is to say, fallen man was obviously still lost.

Hence—to come to our second point—fallen man was cursed. In assigning punishment for the original sin, the Lord apparently accepted the order of guilt assigned by Adam and Eve. Accordingly, the snake was the first to be punished, then the woman, and finally the man (3:14–15).

The first word of God's verdict is "cursed" ('arur), because an historical curse is the lasting effect of the Fall. The Semitic root of this expression, 'rr, is found in Akkadian, Ethiopian, and Arabic—in addition to Hebrew. Pronounced out loud, the word sounds a lot, in fact, like a roar. Well, I suppose it should, because both words, 'arur and "roar" (from the Old English root ra) refer to the same thing—a loud and frightening expression of anger. Long before its first written record on Akkadian temple inscriptions, it is obvious that the root 'rr was an onomatopoeia, a word that imitated a sound, in this case the sound of a lion.

Thus, to be "cursed" (another word, we note, that preserves the same guttural ur sound) means to receive a decree of irate and radical disapproval.

It signifies expulsion from God's society and communion. Moreover, it is of the nature of a curse that it is effective simply by being pronounced.

The curse incurred by fallen man was related to the very earth from which he was taken: "Cursed is the ground ... In the sweat of your face you shall eat bread till you return to the ground from which you were taken. Earth you are, and to earth you shall return." The curse, that is to say, was man's mortality. What Adam handed on was domination by death; "sin reigned in death" (Romans 5:21). By reason of Adam's Fall, man without redemption is under the reign of death and corruption, because "the reign of death [*regnum mortis*] operates only in the corruption of the flesh" (Tertullian, *On the Resurrection* 47).

This is what Adam bequeathed to his offspring, "the reign of death." To die without the grace of redemption is to die eternally. This is the real curse of death, because to die such a death is to be "lost" in a most radical way, lost in the sense of putting oneself beyond the possibility of being found.

Excursus:
First & Second Birth

In biblical history the Lord gives us, not only the definitive revelation of Himself, but also the conclusive revelation of man. That is to say, divine revelation addresses not only the question, "Who is God?" but also the question, "What is man?" I suggest it is useful for Christians to reflect on the unique character of the Bible's answer to this question, because we take our biblical anthropology so much for granted that we fail to count it among those things that many prophets and kings have desired to see but have not seen.

Without divine revelation there are all sorts of theories about man, and in fact the Christian Gospel was obliged to contend with certain of those theories.

One such theory, for instance, claimed (and still does) that "human nature does not change." This theory is understandably attractive, because it provides a sense of universality among human beings and a sense of continuity throughout history. Indeed, as applied to a specified, narrow range of human experiences, we can even call it true.

Yet, if we adhere to the full anthropology of divine revelation, it is strictly speaking not true that "human nature does not change." Indeed, it is the very business of divine revelation to cause human nature to change.

First, humanity begins with an act of change by the very fact of its creation. Thus, St. Gregory of Nyssa, in one of the Christian Church's earliest attempts at a systematic theology, wrote of Creation in general, "Everything that exists through creation is connected with change inasmuch as existence itself originates in change, the non-existing passing into existence by the divine power" (*Oratio Catechetica Magna* 6). Lest we imagine that this general principle of change in creation does not pertain to humanity as such, St. Gregory writes elsewhere of the creation of man, "The created nature cannot exist without change, because its very transition from non-existence to existence is a kind of motion and change of non-being altered into being by the divine will" (*De Opificio Hominis* 16.12).

Humanity takes its rise, then, not from a fixed *esse* but from a dynamic *fieri*; human nature is a "becoming" more than a "being." It is not locked into a defining set of rigid conditions. On the contrary, human nature always bears within itself the "becoming" that marked its very origin. Man has an essentially changeable nature.

Obviously it is impossible for humanity to "remember" that primeval transition from nothing to something, any more than an individual man remembers his own entrance into being. We know of this mystery of our Creation only because it is revealed to us.

Second, this mystery of our original "becoming" is revealed to us in yet another act of becoming, that divine intervention in which our human nature is further altered—namely, our adoption in Christ, the outpouring of the Holy Spirit, whereby we declare "Abba, Father" and "Jesus is Lord."

Our human nature itself is altered by that divine act that makes us sharers in the glory of the Lord, "being transformed into the same image from glory to glory, just as by the Spirit of the Lord" (2 Corinthians 3:18). This is the alteration of our humanity whereby we become "partakers of the divine nature" (2 Peter 1:4), and this is what it means to be "born again."

The man who has not been thus reborn remains ignorant of the very conditions of his first birth. Until he passes through this second "becoming" (genesthe—2 Peter 1:4), man is deceived even about his own humanity. He imagines human nature to be defined, closed, sufficient, and unchanging, but it is no such thing. The true destiny of human nature is not determined by man's first creation but by the renewal of his being in Christ.

As a sharer in the divine nature, the human being is made a child of God, so when he addresses God as "our Father," it is no metaphor, no figure of speech. His nature itself, always open to change, has been transformed by the outpouring of the Holy Spirit. He is truly God's child. He now regards God through the eyes of Christ and addresses God with the voice of Christ.

This is divine revelation's further answer, then, to the question, "What is man?" In his rebirth, man's very nature has been subsumed into the life of God, sharing by divine grace (*energeia*) in Christ's relationship to the Father, a temple of the Holy Spirit, a partaker of the divine nature.

⌒ GENESIS 4 ⌒

The first recorded sacrifices in Holy Scripture are conducted *after* the Fall, indicating that fallen man felt a primeval prompting to worship God in this way. Thus Augustine writes, "And how ancient a part of God's worship sacrifice is, those two brothers, Cain and Abel, sufficiently show, of whom God rejected the elder's sacrifice and looked favorably on the younger's" (*The City of God* 10.4).

Genesis does not indicate why God favored Abel's sacrifice, while rejecting that of Cain. For the answer to this question we must go to Hebrews 11:4: "By faith Abel offered to God a more excellent sacrifice than Cain, through which he obtained witness that he was righteous, God testifying of his gifts." We also observe that this is the first of many biblical instances where God chooses the younger son over the elder (Isaac over Ishmael, Jacob over Esau, Joseph and David over their older brothers, and so forth).

In verse 7 of the Hebrew text, the Lord describes evil as "lying at the door" in wait for Cain. Temptation is portrayed as lurking for a man, stalking him, and Cain is exhorted to vigilance, lest he be taken by it. The Hebrew participle for "lying" here, *robesh*, may be better translated as "crouching." It is related to the name of a god in Assyro-Babylonian literature known as Rabishu, who is described as crouching along the road, endeavoring to waylay the traveler. Cain is warned not to fool with it; it is dangerous. Cain's mother, after all, had made the big mistake of dialoguing with the snake. Satan, however, invariably wins over those who discuss things with him. Or, as we read in the Wisdom of Sirach 21:2, "Flee from sin as you would from the presence of a snake, / For if you approach it, it will bite you."

Cain pays no heed, nonetheless, and goes on to kill his brother (vv. 8–10). The first sin leads to the second. The original alienation in chapter 3 becomes the murder in chapter 4. Jealousy and violence are the proper products of that first act of infidelity. Cain, the first human being begotten of human parents, is also the first murderer. This murder was not committed in a fit of passion. Cain showed, by his response to God in verse 9, that he had closed off his heart to God. His disrespect for God was the foundation on which his murder was based. He could not have killed unless he had isolated himself from God. Moreover, by this murder Cain alienated himself from the very ground on which he walked (vv. 11–12). He had begun as a farmer, but now he is alienated from the soil. He has assumed, by his sin, the impossible task of being a wandering farmer. The foundational reason for Cain's alienation from the earth and his fellowmen is his alienation from God (v. 16).

At this point a new element enters the scene, vengeance. Cain is afraid of the retaliation that may be visited on his head because of his murder of Abel (v. 14). Violence begets violence. God's reply to Cain in verse 15 is reassuring to Cain himself, but it further extends the domain of violence. If Cain is killed, the vengeance will be sevenfold!

Then comes the building of the first city (v. 17), and it is manifestly ironical that this first great effort at this exercise of social cooperation was inaugurated by a murderer! What is said of clothing seems also true of what we may call "urban life." God did not, at the beginning, place man in a city but in a garden. The city was fallen man's idea. The first city was founded by the first murderer. Indeed, the first city was founded by the first fratricide, a fact that becomes the most ironical of archetypes. The irony was certainly not lost on St. Augustine, who commented at some length on the manifest travesty that such a great enterprise of brotherly cooperation should be started by a man who killed his brother. In his lengthy *The City of God*, the saintly bishop of Hippo went on to compare Cain's founding of the city of Enoch to the founding of the city of Rome by Romulus, who had killed Remus, his own brother. Man's efforts, that is to say, are constructed with the elements of their own deterioration. Merely human efforts only disguise man's plight for a while. The heart of all evil is alienation from God, so any society founded on that alienation has already drunk poison. It will surely die.

It is abundantly curious that Cain's descendants take up, among other things, the crafting of musical instruments. This is another example of a cultural form conceived in evil, but which God takes special care to redeem. What we said about clothing and urban life also applies to musical instruments. Originally crafted by a descendant of Cain, they do not look promising at first. Moreover, there has often been something a bit problematic about such music, morally considered. When King Nebuchadnezzar employed "the sound of the trumpet, the pipe, the harp, the four-stringed instrument, the psaltery, the symphony, and every kind of music" (Daniel 3:5) for his idolatrous purposes, it was not the last instance when instrumental music served to deflect men from the worship of the true God. Yet, in fact, God rather early designated musical instruments as appropriate to His own worship in the tabernacle and the temple. And, once again, in the final book of the Bible, we find heaven to be a place resonating with the sounds of trumpet and harp. Moreover, as an added irony, instrumental music is eventually limited so exclusively to the saints in heaven that the damned in hell are forever deprived of such music! The sinful descendants of Cain, the very inventors of harp and flute, will never hear them again, inasmuch as the "sound of harpists, musicians, flutists, and trumpeters shall not be heard in you anymore" (Revelation 18:22). These things are now reserved for the blessed.

Excursus:
The Price of Faith

Not least among the ironies of the Bible is the fact that its very first family was also its first dysfunctional family. For one thing, the boys didn't get along. Fratricide is a useful clue.

The theological source of the problem, certainly, was the sin of the first parents in chapter 3, though the novelist Jessamyn West did offer her own peculiar slant on the point: "Always thought Adam might've handled his boys better if he'd been a boy himself. . . . Worked under a handicap, as it was."

In regard to these two brothers it is ironical, too, that the first man to die was also the first to be murdered. More ironical still, perhaps, he was murdered for his religious faith. "By faith," Holy Scripture tells us, "Abel offered to God a more excellent sacrifice than Cain" (Hebrews 11:4), and "Cain was extremely sorrowful, and his countenance fell." Consumed with rage, he at last "rose up against Abel his brother and killed him" (Genesis 4:5, 8). The first man to die, therefore, perished in testimony to his faith, and it was an angry unbeliever who took his life.

The key to the discernment of the first murder is the prior moral fissure dividing these two men. Murder was the fruit, not the root, of Cain's offense. St. John tells us, "Whoever hates his brother is a murderer" (1 John 3:15). Antecedent to the killing itself, then, the killer was already "of the wicked one" (1 John 3:12). According to Theophilus of Antioch in the second century, it was Satan who "moved his brother, called Cain, and made him kill his brother Abel. And thus the beginning of death [*arche thanatou*] came into this world" (*To Autolycus* 2.29). In the following century, the Alexandrian Origen remarked that "evil did not begin in Cain when he slew his brother." On the contrary, he said, he was a bad man all along, and "God read his heart." It was simply the case that Cain's "evil became manifest [*eis phaneron elthen*] when he slew Abel" (*On Prayer* 29.18).

While we easily perceive that Cain killed because he was a bad man, it is important to see also that Abel was slain precisely because he was a good man. His goodness was the very reason that Cain took his life. St. John affirms it: "And why did he murder him? Because his works were evil and his brother's righteous" (1 John 3:12). While it is said of Cain that "he perished in anger for murdering his brother" (Wisdom of Solomon 10:3), of Abel we are told that "he obtained witness that he was righteous" (Hebrews 11:4).

Thus commences the Bible's reading of history as a prolonged chronicle of "all the righteous blood shed on the earth, from the blood of righteous Abel" (Matthew 23:35). The saga of persecution begins with "The voice of your brother's blood cries out to Me from the ground" (Genesis 4:10) and ends with "How long, O Lord, holy and true, until You judge and avenge our blood on those who dwell on the earth?" (Revelation 6:10).

Abel, then, though dead since the dawn of his-tory, "still speaks" (Hebrews 11:4). Origen commented, "Let us recognize that what was said of Abel, who was slain by the homicidal and unjust Cain, pertains to all whose blood is unjustly shed. We may consider as pertinent to each of the martyrs the words, 'Your brother's blood cries out to me from the earth,' because from the ground their blood shouts out to God" (*Exhortation to Martyrdom* 50).

If Adam is the Old Testament's first type (*typos*) of the Christ to come (Romans 5:14; 1 Corinthians 15:45), the death of Abel is rightly regarded as the first foreshadowing sign of Christ's death on the Cross. Jesus Himself laid the foundation for this symbolism by declaring that "all the righteous blood shed on the earth, from the blood of righteous Abel," would come upon the generation of those who crucified Him (Matthew 23:35). For this reason, St. Augustine believed that the death of Christ was represented in the figure of Abel (*The City of God* 15.18).

The author of Hebrews, who described Abel's blood crying out to God from the earth, went on to invoke this same image with respect to Jesus' own blood. The blood of Jesus, he wrote, "speaks better things than *that of* Abel" (12:24). Whereas Abel's blood cried out demanding revenge, the blood of Jesus, who is called here "the Mediator of the new covenant," invokes the divine mercy for sinners. Such is the blood in which we have access to "the city of the living God, the heavenly Jerusalem" (12:22).

༈ GENESIS 5 ༈

In this first biblical genealogy we draw special attention to the figure of Enoch. After the Epistle to the Hebrews gives its initial definition of faith as "the substance of things hoped for, the evidence of things not seen" (11:1), there follows the famous list of the "great cloud of witnesses" (12:1), those "elders" who "obtained a good testimony" by exemplifying such faith (11:2).

One can hardly fail to observe in this list the strong emphasis on death with respect to this saving faith. Throughout Hebrews 11 faith has to do with how one dies, and "these all died in faith" (11:13). This emphasis on death in the context of faith renders very interesting the inclusion of Enoch among the list of faith's exemplars, because Enoch departed this world in some way other than death. Indeed, in the genealogy here in chapter 5, the verb "died" occurs eight times with respect to the patriarchs from Adam to Lamech, but in the case of Enoch, "the seventh from Adam" (Jude 14), our text says simply he "was well-pleasing to God, and was not found [*ouk eurisketo*], for God translated [*metetheken*] him" (v. 24).

By way of commentary on this passage, the Epistle to the Hebrews says, "By faith Enoch was taken away [*metethe*] so that he did not see death, 'and was not found [*ouk eurisketo*], because God had taken [*metetheken*] him'; for before he was taken [*metatheseos*] he had this testimony, that he pleased [*euariestekenai*] God" (11:5). That ancient "testimony," cited here in the Epistle to the Hebrews, is found in the Wisdom of Solomon, where Enoch is thus described:

[He was] pleasing [*euarestos*] to God and loved by Him,
And while living among sinners he was taken up
   [*metetethe*].
He was caught up lest evil change his understanding
Or deceit deceive his soul.
For envy arising from lack of judgment obscures what
   is good,
And a whirling of desire undermines an innocent heart.
He was made perfect [*teleotheis*],
For in a short time he fulfilled long years,
For his soul was pleasing [*areste*] to the Lord;
Therefore, He took him early from the midst of evil."
(4:10–14)

Such is the biblical witness about the "short time" that Enoch spent on this earth (a mere 365 years, according to v. 23). Unlike the other heroes listed in Hebrews 11, Enoch did not die in faith, for the unusual reason that he did not die at all. He nonetheless deserved a place in that heroic list, we are told, because "he pleased God" by his faith. Thus, when we believers "come boldly to the throne of grace" (Hebrews 4:16), when we approach "the general assembly and church of the firstborn *who are* registered in heaven," there stands Enoch among "the spirits of just men made perfect [*teteleiomenon*]" (12:23).

Living before Noah, Abraham, and Moses, Enoch was participant in none of the covenants associated with these men. Not a single line of Holy Scripture was yet written for him to read. Much less did Enoch ever hear the message of salvation preached by the apostles. Yet, he was so pleasing to God by his faith as to be snatched away before his time, not suffering that common lot of death from which the Almighty spared not even His own Son.

What, exactly, did Enoch *believe*, then, that he should be such a champion of faith, an example for the Church until the end of time? The Epistle to the Hebrews explains: "But without faith *it is* impossible to please *Him*, for he who comes to God must believe that He is, and *that* He is a rewarder of those who diligently seek Him" (11:6). This was the sum total of all that Enoch's faith told Him—God's existence and his own duty to seek God in order to obtain the singular blessing that Holy Scripture ascribes to him. It is the Bible's portrayal of Enoch, then, that affords us some hope for the salvation of those millions of human beings who must pass their lives on that bare minimum of theological information, for which Enoch rendered such a marvelous account.

PART TWO
THE NOAH CYCLE

⚘

᛫ GENESIS 6 ᛫

In the New Testament the Deluge, to which these next five chapters of Genesis are devoted, is understood as a type of baptism. Thus, St. Peter, writing of Christ's descent into hell after His death, goes on immediately to treat of Noah, the Deluge, our own baptisms, and the Lord's Resurrection. For the early Christians, these are all components of the same Mystery of regeneration:

> For Christ also suffered once for sins, the just for the unjust, that He might bring us to God, being put to death in the flesh but made alive by the Spirit, by whom also He went and preached to the spirits in prison, who formerly were disobedient, when once the Divine longsuffering waited in the days of Noah, while *the* ark was being prepared, in which a few, that is, eight souls, were saved through water. There is also an antitype which now saves us—baptism (not the removal of the filth of the flesh, but the answer of a good conscience toward God), through the resurrection of Jesus Christ (1 Peter 3:18–21).

We must be baptized because we are sinners, and our sins are washed away in baptism: "Arise and be baptized, and wash away your sins, calling on the name of the Lord" (Acts 22:16). Or earlier, "Repent, and let every one of you be baptized in the name of Jesus Christ for the remission of sins" (2:38).

Like the Deluge, there is something destructive about baptism. Baptism has been given to the world because the world is full of sin, and through this water we are delivered from the world of sin.

Whether we speak of the baptismal type in the Deluge, therefore, or of the fulfillment of that type in baptism itself, we must begin with sin.

Thus, the Deluge account begins with a description of a world full of sin (vv. 1–5, 11–13), ending with God's sorrow at having made man and His resolve to destroy man from the earth (vv. 6–7). Noah alone has pleased God (v. 8), so God will spare Noah and his family. God commands Noah to build the ark, and He remains patient a while longer while the ark is being constructed (1 Peter 3:20).

Then Noah and his family wait quietly in the ark for seven days, until the rains come. The rains come "after seven days" (v. 10), which is to say, on the eighth day. The number seven, reminiscent of the week of Creation, signifies the old world, whereas the number eight serves as a symbol of the New Creation. In the second century, St. Justin Martyr remarked that "the mystery of saved men happened in the Deluge, because righteous Noah, along with other human beings at the Deluge—namely, his own wife, his three children, and the wives of his sons—who were eight persons in number, contained a symbol of the number of the eighth day, in which our Christ appeared, having risen from the dead" (*Dialogue with Trypho* 138.1).

Excursus:
Noah & Moses

In the third century, Cyprian of Carthage affirmed that "the one ark of Noah was a figure of the one Church" during the flood, that "baptism of the world in which it was purified and redeemed" (*Letters* 68.2). Jerome (*Letters* 133) and Augustine (*Against Faustus* 12.17) said much the same in the early fifth century. Various combinations of this imagery are ubiquitous in patristic and liturgical texts.

The root of such symbolism is found in the Old Testament's own portrayal of Noah's ark. Genesis calls it a *tevah*, a word used in only one other place in the Hebrew Scriptures, namely, to designate the little box in which the infant Moses floated on the Nile.

Indeed, the juxtaposition of the two stories seems clearly intentional if we examine the manifest similarities between them. First, in respect to both Noah and Moses, the *tevah* is a floating container that preserves life from the peril of drowning. That is to say, the threat comes from water. Second, in each case the container is daubed with pitch to keep out the threatening water (6:14; Exodus 2:3). Third, both stories contribute to the ongoing biblical theme of God's deliverance of His servants in times of crisis.

There is an even subtler element here, however. The word *tevah* is not Hebrew; it is Egyptian, in which language it may designate a box, a chest, even a coffin. Its use in only these two biblical passages cries out for an explanation.

Why does the Bible borrow this strange word and then use it in only these two places? That is to say, why does the Bible not state, in plain Hebrew, that Noah built a boat (*'abarah*) or a ship (*'oniyyah*)? And why, when Moses was put into that little container made of reeds, is the thing not simply called, in plain Hebrew, a box (*'aron*) or a basket (*tene*)? Why do these two stories in Genesis and Exodus make such a point of employing an improbable, alien word not otherwise found in the Bible?

I can think of a single reasonable answer. Namely, that the biblical author had in mind to tie these two accounts together in a very explicit way, so that the correspondence between them would be unmistakable. The setting of the Moses story may have suggested the use of the Egyptian noun *tevah*. There stands out, in short, a clear literary parallel between the stories of old Noah near the beginning of Genesis and young Moses near the beginning of Exodus.

This correspondence will be evident to those who regularly read the Bible in Hebrew. For example, the medieval rabbinic scholar Rashi called attention to it in his commentary on Genesis (though not, curiously, in his commentary on Exodus).

However, the important literary and theological relationship between Genesis 6—9 and Exodus 2 is all but obliterated in many translations, starting even with the Septuagint and the Vulgate. More recently, the English Standard Version, while leaving Noah in his "ark," plops poor little baby Moses down in a mere "basket." On the other hand, it is one of the merits of the King James Bible that it employs the word "ark" (from the Latin *arca*, meaning box or chest) in both places, thus explicitly tying the two passages together.

And they certainly should be studied together, joining Moses with Noah, and the Exodus account with the narrative of the Flood. As Noah in his *tevah* saved the human race and the animals from utter destruction, so the baby Moses, preserved in a tiny *tevah* of his own, became the deliverer of the Hebrews. Indeed, Moses' very name, which means "drawn from the water," is a foreshadowing of Israel's deliverance from Pharaoh's army at the Red Sea. Moses is a kind of new Noah. In his *tevah* at the beginning of this story, he makes his own personal exodus, as it were, a promise of the one to come.

The themes in both stories, finally, symbolize the Sacrament of Baptism, in which God's people, even today, are "drawn from the water."

ᖷ: GENESIS 7 :ᖷ

Noah's construction of the ark represented his faith, according to the Epistle to the Hebrews: "By faith Noah, being divinely warned of things not yet seen, moved with godly fear, prepared an ark for the saving of his household, by which he condemned the world and became heir of the righteousness which is according to faith" (11:7).

Noah not only lived in righteousness; he also preached righteousness to his contemporaries. The Apostle Peter referred to Noah as "a preacher of righteousness" (2 Peter 2:5), and late in the first century Clement of Rome wrote that "Noah preached repentance, and those who heeded him were saved" (*Epistle to the Corinthians* 7.6). Evidently, however, their number included only members of his own family!

This picture of Noah as a somewhat unsuccessful preacher came to the early Christians from Jewish lore. Flavius Josephus wrote of Noah's relationship to his contemporaries in this way:

> Noah was most uncomfortable with their actions, and, not at all happy with their conduct, he persuaded them to improve their dispositions and their actions. Seeing, nonetheless, that they did not obey him but remained slaves to their own wicked desires, he feared that they would slay him, together with his wife and children, as well as the spouses of the latter, so he departed out of that land. (*Antiquities* 13.1)

Unlike Noah's contemporaries, we ourselves hearken to his preaching. That is to say, we submit to this new baptismal flood because we repent at the witness of Noah. Baptism presupposes and requires this repentance of our sins, this conversion of our hearts to the apostolic word of Noah. In repentance we plunge ourselves into the deeper mystery of Noah's flood, which is the death and Resurrection of Christ our Lord (Romans 6:3; Colossians 2:12).

ᴄ: Genesis 8 :ᴐ

The dove sent out by Noah is also rich in symbolism. Since, as we have seen, baptism is the fulfillment of that mystery of which the flood was a type, we should rather expect the dove to appear in the New Testament descriptions of baptism, and indeed it does. At the baptism of our Lord, the Holy Spirit assumes that form in order to confirm the testimony of the Father, who proclaims Jesus His beloved Son. Thus, St. Cyril of Jerusalem wrote:

Some say that, just as salvation came in the time of Noah by the wood and the water, and as the dove came back to Noah in the evening with an olive branch, so, they say, the Holy Spirit descended on the true Noah, the author of the new creation, when the spiritual dove came upon Him at His baptism, to demonstrate that He it is who, by the wood of the cross, confers salvation on believers, and who, by His death at eventide, conferred on the world the grace of salvation.

The ark, on which the Spirit descends, is a symbol of the Church, the vessel of salvation. In the ironical words of Cyprian of Carthage in the mid-third century, "If anyone who was outside the ark could have escaped, so would he escape who was outside the Church" (*On the Unity of the Catholic Church* 6). That is to say, it is impossible to be saved outside of the Church, because the name of Jesus Christ is the only name under heaven given us by which we must be saved, and the Ark-Church is the vessel which holds all of those who call upon the name of the Lord Jesus Christ unto their salvation.

We may summarize the Christian teaching on the story of the Flood with these words of John Chrysostom in the second half of the fourth century:

> The narrative of the Flood is a mystery, and its details are a type of things to come. The ark is the Church; Noah is Christ; the dove, the Holy Spirit; the olive branch, the divine goodness. As in the midst of the sea, the ark protected those who were within it, so the Church saves those who are saved. (*Homily on Lazarus* 6)

ᔆ GENESIS 9 ᔆ

The word "covenant" (*berith*), which appeared in 6:18 for the first time in Holy Scripture, is now taken up and developed. The earliest explicit account of God's covenant, that is to say, is the covenant with Noah. The second divine covenant, which we shall see in chapters 15 and 17, is God's covenant with Abraham. In Genesis the idea of God's covenant is found in only these two narratives.

The first, the Noachic covenant here in chapter 9, is God's covenant with the entire world and with mankind in particular. The second, the Abrahamic covenant especially as described in chapter 17, is God's more particular covenant with the descendants of Abraham, which will be further defined as the biblical narrative continues. There are several significant theological features shared by these two covenant narratives in Genesis, features reflected in a distinctive vocabulary that distinguishes them from the other covenants recorded in Holy Scripture.

One of the distinguishing features shared by these two covenants, in chapters 9 and 17, is the choice of verbs employed to predicate it. In most of Holy Scripture, the verb used for "making" a covenant is *karat*, literally "to cut." Although the initiative in the covenant is always God's, the verb *karat* does suggest something of a mutual agreement between two parties. In fact, both the verb *karat* and the noun *berith* were commonly employed in the ancient world to designate political treaties. Examples of this usage are the treaty between Abraham and Abimelech in 21:27, and the treaty between Isaac and Abimelech in 26:28. In God's covenant with Abraham in 15:18, moreover, *karat* is the verb employed for the making of the covenant, as is the case in most of the Hebrew Scriptures (for instance, Deuteronomy 5:2).

In these Genesis covenants of God with Noah and Abraham, however, two other verbs are employed: *natan*, "to give" (9:12; 17:2), and *haqim*, "to establish" (9:9, 11; 17:7). The first of these verbs emphasizes the gratuity, the generosity, of God's act in making the covenant; it is pure, unmerited grace. This is why, in each case, God calls it "*My* covenant" (9:15; 17:7). The second verb places the accent on God's resolve in the covenant; God Himself will not break the covenant. Each of these covenants is a perpetual pledge of hope for the future.

A second distinguishing feature of these two covenants in chapters 9 and 17 is the *'oth berith*, "the sign of the covenant," a distinctive symbol of each covenant. In the case of Noah, the *'oth berith* is the rainbow (9:12–17), and in the case of Abraham it is circumcision (17:1).

In the covenant with Noah, the function of the rainbow as a "sign" is to cause God to "remember" His covenant (9:15–16). The covenant sign serves as a reminder, as it were, a "memorial," a *zik-karon* in Hebrew, an *anamnesis* in Greek. This theme will be taken up later on in Holy Scripture, when Jesus describes God's definitive covenant with the Church in terms of an *anamnesis* (Luke 22:19; 1 Corinthians 11:24–25). The Lord's Supper, that is to say, is not simply an occasion for Christians to remember Jesus and His saving work on our behalf; as a "sign of the covenant," the rite of breaking the bread and sharing the cup is even more the ineffable *'oth berith* to God Himself, in which He is called upon to "remember" the redemption that He has definitively given and established with us in the Lord Jesus. This is why the Church's celebration of the Holy Eucharist is the defining act of her existence.

With respect to these characteristics of the covenant with Noah, something should also be said of the Mosaic covenant as described in Exodus 31. This latter text ties the covenant on Sinai to both the Sabbath rest and the covenant with Abraham. The "sign" of the Mosaic covenant is the Sabbath, which is described in terms very reminiscent of the covenant with Noah here in chapter 9. The Sabbath is the sign (*'oth*) between God and Israel (Exodus 31:13, 17), much as the covenant with Noah is between God and "all flesh." More specifically, the Sabbath is the sign of Israel's "perpetual covenant" (*berith 'olam*) with God (Exodus 31:16). Thus, in the Exodus account we find the same vocabulary used with respect to the Sabbath that we have here in chapter 9 to describe the symbolic function of the rainbow.

It is instructive to observe three points with respect to these similarities between Genesis 9 and Exodus 31. First, they are intentional and deliberately invite a theological comparison between the two covenants as they appear in the history of salvation, the covenant with mankind at the conclusion of the Flood and the covenant with Israel at the conclusion of the Exodus.

Second, both "signs" in these covenants are built on the structure of nature itself. This is true not only of the rainbow, but also of the Sabbath. It is clearly the teaching of Genesis 2:2–3 that the Sabbath pertains to the natural structure of that creature known as "time." Thus, each of these covenants is signified (that is to say, marked with a sign) by a component that God placed in created nature.

Third, in the case of the covenant with Noah following the Flood, God Himself preserves the sign of the covenant. He places

His bow in the heavens (9:13). In the Mosaic covenant, in contrast, the maintenance of the covenant sign depends on Israel. It is Israel that is charged to preserve the Sabbath. Thus, the similarities between these two covenants introduce also a contrast.

◠: Genesis 10 :◡

Already at the end of the previous chapter we found that all was not well among the sons of Noah, and the tensions of that chapter will be developed extensively in the rest of the biblical story. More particularly, the discussion of the variety of nations in the present chapter prepares the way for the account of the diversity of tongues in chapter 11.

The present chapter describes the fortunes of Noah's three sons, with a view to the later stories of the Exodus and the conquest of the Promised Land. The Egyptians and Canaanites, after all, are the descendants of Ham, while the Israelites are the descendents of Shem.

The present list of the nations, however, seems more preoccupied with geography than ethnicity. We note that the descendants of Shem (still called Semites) mainly inhabit the Fertile Crescent, while the offspring of Ham inhabit areas to the south and southwest of the Fertile Crescent, and the children of Japheth live to the northwest, in the area of the Turkish peninsula and the Aegean Sea. That is to say, this list covers roughly the three landmasses that contain the Mediterranean Basin: southern Europe, western Asia, and northern Africa.

About seventy nations are listed. We remember, in this respect, that Jesus sent out exactly that number of apostles (Luke 10:1), a number indicating the universality of their mission to "make disciples of *all* nations."

◠: Genesis 11 :◡

In spite of the national diversities outlined in the previous chapter, all of mankind, up to this point, speaks with a common tongue (v. 1).

The construction of Babel, the second city to be founded in

the Bible, prompts us to recall the moral ambiguity of the first city, founded by the world's first fratricide (4:17). Babel, like that first city, represents the development of technology (v. 3; 4:22). The tower of Babel symbolizes man's arrogance and his rebellion against the authority of God. Not trusting God's promise never again to destroy the world by flood (9:15), the men of Babel decide to build this tower as a sort of insurance policy against God's punishment. Its construction, therefore, is of a piece with all the earlier rebellions against God we have seen, starting in chapter 3.

God's response is twofold. It is both a punishment of the rebels and a preventative measure against their becoming even worse. That is to say, even God's punishment is an act of mercy.

In the more general symbolism of Holy Scripture, Babel also represents Babylon, the city of power and godless rebellion, which is overthrown definitively in the Book of Revelation. There is a symbolic identity, therefore, uniting the present story to the destruction of Babylon described in Revelation 17 and 18. This city represents any political and economic establishment characterized by arrogance and the love of power.

Its punishment by the division of tongues was especially appropriate. Augustine of Hippo comments on this chapter:

> As the tongue is the instrument of domination, in it pride was punished, so that man, who refused to understand God when He gave His commands, should also be misunderstood when he gave commands. Thus was dissolved their conspiracy, because each man withdrew from those who could not understand and banded with those whose speech he found intelligible. So the nations were divided according to their languages and scattered over the face of the earth, as seemed good to God, who accomplished this in hidden ways that we cannot understand. (*The City of God* 16.4)

PART THREE
THE ABRAHAM CYCLE

ॐ

⌁ GENESIS 12 ⌁

The genealogy of Shem's descendants, at the end of chapter 11, pre-pared us for this beginning of the story of Abram, whom we first find at the city of Ur, in the extreme southeast end of the Fertile Crescent. That genealogy also introduced other aspects of the later story. It told us, for instance, of the barrenness of Abram's wife (11:30), which is a detail crucial to the later narrative. Likewise, it introduced Lot, Abram's nephew, who will appear at significant points in the story later on. Similarly, it told of those relatives who were left behind; these, too, will be important in later aspects of the story.

The first migration goes from Ur up to Haran, at the very top and center of the Fertile Crescent (11:31), and from there Abram's com-pany proceeds to migrate south and west (vv. 5, 9). Passing through Canaan, also known in the Bible as Palestine (the Roman name for Philistia), Abram arrives in Egypt, the southwestern extremity of the Fertile Crescent. All of this migration is in obedience to God's call (cf. Acts 7:1–5; Hebrews 11:8–10). Nor was Abram a young man at this point; he was already seventy-five years old (v. 4).

Abram's brief sojourn in Egypt (vv. 10–20) prefigures Israel's later experience of that country. Thus, he is driven into Egypt by a famine in Canaan (v. 10), exactly as Israel will be in the final chapters of Genesis (41:57—42:2). In Egypt Abram encounters Pharaoh, king of Egypt, as Israel will do near the end of Genesis and at the beginning of Exodus. Indeed, one already observes Pharaoh to be a rapacious, threatening, high-handed man of arbitrary behavior, exactly as we will find the other Pharaoh encountered by Moses.

Excursus:
Exodus in Genesis

One is impressed with the ways in which the Book of Genesis prepares its readers for the Book of Exodus. This should not be surprising, because the contents of Exodus were probably more important to Ezra and the other biblical editors than were the stories in Genesis. Exodus, after all, contains the beginning of the first of the laws given to Israel at Mount Sinai.

It is worth remarking, in this respect, that our reading of the Bible today differs considerably from that of the ancient rabbis who assembled and edited the Sacred Text. Many modern readers, who delight in the exciting stories throughout Genesis, sometimes find themselves getting rather bored and bogged down when they encounter all the rules and ordinances that fill the second half of Exodus. Indeed, those numerous regulations in Exodus, Leviticus, Numbers, and Deuteronomy, if not skipped altogether by modern readers, are often read with little interest. Many a copy of the Bible, one suspects, is encumbered with a bookmark that never moved past Exodus 21 or so.

This was not the case for Ezra and his editorial associates. Doubtless the ancients loved those narratives in Genesis, but their major interest was in the rules and regulations that followed them. For them, the important thing was the Law, the Torah, the expression of God's will and mind revealed on Mount Sinai.

This perspective is clear in the Hebrew canon itself. Even the Book of Genesis is subsumed there under the heading "Torah," the first of those books called simply "The Five" (*Chumash*), or the "five fifths of the Law." That is to say, in the Hebrew canon Genesis serves as an introduction, a preamble, to the whole Torah. It is an integral part of the Law. Thus, we recall that St. Paul, when he sought to "establish the law," immediately appealed to Genesis (Romans 3:31—4:3).

If the entire thrust of Genesis is directed towards the giving of the Torah, it makes sense to expect anticipations of the Book of Exodus already in the Book of Genesis.

In fact, these anticipations begin rather early. As soon as the Flood is over, for example, we learn of the sin of Ham, the forefather of those very Egyptians who will eventually enslave Israel (9:22).

Among Ham's other descendants were the people of Babel (10:10), who undertook the first recorded example of brick construction (11:3). With those bricks, let us remember, those descendants of Ham endeavored to raise the famous tower at Babel, an act of defiance against God.

That early account of rebellious brick-making prepares the reader for the later story of Egypt's various building projects, which will form the context of the opening of the Book of Exodus. In fact, the compulsory making of bricks was Pharaoh's way of oppressing God's people (Exodus 1:10–11; 3:7; 5:6–16). The arrogant monarch confronted by Moses was nothing if not a rebellious builder with bricks.

That earlier building project at Babel anticipates, then, the future building projects of Pharaoh in Egypt. Both building projects use the same material—bricks, a word that only rarely appears in the rest of the Hebrew Bible.

In Holy Scripture both Babel and Egypt represent pretty much the same thing, the worldly, idolatrous city rising in defiance against the true God, especially by its advanced technology. Baked bricks are an example of the latter.

Pharaoh's defeat in Exodus is also prophesied in the Book of Genesis, both by an explicit message

to Abraham in a mystic vision (15:14; Acts 7:6–7),
and by the story of Pharaoh's abduction of Sarah in
chapter 12. This latter text merits close examination
with respect to our theme.

First, Abraham and Sarah are driven into Egypt
by famine (12:10), exactly as famine will later be
the cause of Israel's sojourn there, which sets the
scene for the Exodus (45:6–11). Second, when
Abraham and Sarah arrive in Egypt they encounter
the high-handed, arbitrary, and menacing behavior
of a Pharaoh (12:11–15), just as Moses will. Third,
Abraham deceives and outwits Pharaoh with
double-talk (12:12–16), which is what Moses will do
as well (Exodus 3:18; 7:16; 8:1, 20, 25–28). Fourth,
Abraham's encounter with Pharaoh leads to plagues
inflicted on Egypt (Genesis 12:17). This same word,
"plagues" (nega'im), will be used in the Book of Exodus to portray the punishments endured by Egypt
because of Pharaoh's hardness of heart (Exodus
11:1). Finally, like Moses and the Israelites (Exodus
3:20–22; 11:1–3; 12:35–36), Abraham is enriched
with the spoils of Egypt when he leaves the place
(Genesis 12:16, 20).

In summary, the various elements of Abraham's
brief sojourn in Egypt prefigure the drama of the
Exodus: the famine, the arrogance of Pharaoh, the
superior wisdom of the prophet, God's intervention
by sending the plagues, the vindication of the Chosen
People and their departure from Egypt, enriched
with its spoils. Abraham thus foreshadows Moses.
Genesis prefigures Exodus.

❧ GENESIS 13 ❧

When Abram left Egypt, he and his family were very wealthy, because of Pharaoh's generosity to someone he was trying to gain as

a brother-in-law. Now Abram and Lot find that the sheer size of their flocks requires them to live apart (vv. 1–7). The story of their separation (vv. 8–13) demonstrates Abram's humility in giving his younger relative the choice of the land (v. 9), while he himself takes what is left. This humble action of Abram illustrates the meaning of the Lord's saying that the meek shall inherit the earth. Abraham's descendants, not Lot's, will inherit all this land. In this story we discern the non-assertive quality of Abram's faith. He is not only meek; he is also a peacemaker. Meekness and peacemaking are qualities of the man of faith.

Lot serves in this story as a kind of foil to Abram. The meek and peaceful Abram takes what is left, whereas Lot, obviously having failed to do a proper survey of the neighborhood, chooses to live in Sodom. This was to prove one of the worst real estate choices in history.

The present chapter closes with God's solemn asseveration to Abram, promising him the land and the "seed" (vv. 14–18). Unfortunately the rich ambivalence of this latter noun (*zera'* in Hebrew, *sperma* in Greek, *semen* in Latin) is lost in more recent translations that substitute the politically correct but entirely prosaic "descendants" for "seed" (vv. 15–16).

Besides Sodom, two other important Canaanite cities are introduced in this chapter, Bethel (still called Luz at this period—cf. 28:19) and Hebron. Both of these cities will be extremely important in subsequent biblical history, and Abram is credited with making each of them a place of worship (vv. 4, 18).

❧ GENESIS 14 ❧

The Old Testament provides a genealogy, at least in brief, for most of its *dramatis personae*. The clear exception is Melchizedek, who suddenly enters the biblical story in this chapter of Genesis and just as abruptly leaves it. Nothing whatever is said of his ancestry, the rest of his life, or his death. Melchizedek simply appears "without father, without mother, without genealogy, having neither beginning of days, nor end of life" (Hebrews 7:3). In fact, chapter 14 tells us only five things about him.

First, Melchizedek was a king. Salem, the city of his kingship, was an old name for Jerusalem (Psalm 76[75]:2, sometimes translated "peace"). Indeed, the Jewish historian, Flavius Josephus, took Melchizedek to be the founder (*ho protos ktisas*) of the holy city (*The Jewish War* 6.438). Speculating on the etymology of Melchizedek's name (*melek-hassedeq*), Josephus calls him a "righteous king" (*basileus dikaios*) (*Antiquities* 1.10.2).

Exploiting the resemblance of the name Salem to the Hebrew word for "peace," *shalom*, the author of the Epistle to the Hebrews calls Melchizedek "king of peace." Like Josephus, he sees etymological symbolism in Melchizedek's own name, calling him "king of righteousness" (*basileus dikaiosynes*) (7:2).

Second, Melchizedek was "the priest of God Most High" (v. 18). In fact, he is the first man to whom Holy Scripture gives the title "priest" (*kohen*), and it is Melchizedek's priesthood that receives the greater attention in the Bible. For example, while the Book of Psalms speaks of the Messiah's kingship as derived from David (Psalms 78[77]:70; 89[88]:3–4, 20, 39, 45; 110[109]:1–3), the Messiah's priesthood is said to be "according to the order of Melchizedek" (110[109]:4).

Melchizedek was "the first to serve as priest to God" (*ierasato to Theo protos*), Josephus wrote, and long before Solomon built a temple at Jerusalem, Melchizedek had already done so (*to hieron protos deimamenos*). Indeed, Josephus traces the very name of Jerusalem (in Greek *Hierosolyma*) to this "priest of Salem" (*hierus Salem*) (*The Jewish War* 6.438).

Following the lead of Psalm 110(109), the author of Hebrews sees in the priesthood of Melchizedek the "order" (*taxsis*) of the definitive priesthood of Christ the Lord (5:6, 10; 6:20; 7:17). The Bible's very silence with respect to the death of that ancient priest of Salem is taken as a prefiguration of the "unchangeable priesthood" (7:24) of God's Son, to whom Melchizedek was "made like" (7:3). The latter was a living prophecy of the definitive Priest who "has become a surety of a better covenant" (7:22).

Third, Abraham gave a tithe to Melchizedek, just as Abraham's children gave tithes to the Levitical priests (7:8–10). That detail argues for the superiority of the "order of Melchizedek" over the "order of Aaron" (7:11).

Fourth, Melchizedek blessed Abraham, saying: "Blessed be Abram of God Most High, Creator of heaven and earth; and blessed be God Most High, who delivered your enemies into your hands" (Genesis 14:19–20). This priestly blessing too indicates the superiority of the "order of Melchizedek," inasmuch as "the lesser is blessed by the better" (Hebrews 7:7).

Fifth, Melchizedek "brought out bread and wine" (Genesis 14:18). His offering of bread and wine, moreover, was recognized as a priestly act; that is to say, Melchizedek did this precisely *because he was* a priest (as is clear in the Septuagint's *en de* and the Vulgate's *erat enim*).

Melchizedek's offering of bread and wine, of course, was a type and prefiguration of what transpired that night when God's priestly Son took the loaf of bread and the cup of wine into His holy and venerable hands and identified them as His Body and Blood. This is how the Christian Church has always interpreted the act of that first priest, Melchizedek, "who gave the wine and bread, the sanctified food, as a type of the Eucharist [*eis typon Eucharistias*]" (Clement of Alexandria, *Stromateis* 4.25). Melchizedek was the "type of Christ, and he offered the same gifts that prefigured the Mystery" (John Chrysostom, *Homilies on Genesis* 36.3). "Who had the bread and wine?" asked Ambrose of Milan. "Not Abraham," he answered, "but Melchizedek. Therefore he is the author of the Sacraments" (*De Sacramentis* 4.10). The living memory of Melchizedek thus abides deeply in the worship of the Christian Church.

❦ GENESIS 15 ❧

This, the first of two accounts of God's covenant with Abram, is arguably the more dramatic and colorful. Here we also find two expressions appearing for the first time in Holy Scripture: (1) "the Word of the Lord came to . . ." (v. 1), and (2) Abram "believed ['*aman*] God, and He accounted it to him for righteousness" (v. 6). That first expression will be especially prominent in the Bible's prophetic literature, and the second, which introduces the theme of righteousness by faith in God's promise, will dominate much of the New Testament, particularly the Pauline corpus. Indeed, St. Paul wrote the first Christian commentary on this verse, Romans 4:1–5.

At this point in the story, Abram is not called upon to *do* anything. He is summoned simply to live by trust in God's promising word. Eventually, of course, he will be called upon to *do* certain things, but the important point that St. Paul sees in this passage is that *already*, before he has done anything, Abram is called righteous. From this fact St. Paul argues that godly righteousness consists radically in that profound trust in God known in the Bible as faith. This *faith* is now explicitly spoken of for the first time in Holy Scripture. Hence, the importance of chapter 15 for Christian theology. This is why Abraham is called "our father" in faith; his faith stands at the door of the history of salvation.

For St. Paul, Abraham's righteousness, prior to the works of the Mosaic covenant, became the point of departure for examining the Christian's relationship to the Law of Moses, which was one of the most difficult and practical questions raised in New Testament times. For example, it was important to St. Paul that Abraham, at this point in the story, has not yet received the command to be circumcised (Romans 4:9–12); that command will not come until chapter 17. That is to say, Abraham was declared righteous *before* circumcision.

❧ GENESIS 16 ❧

Like the precedent referred to in 15:2–4, the "legal fiction" found here in vv. 1–3 (and later on in the Jacob cycle) was never part of Israelite law, though both customs are well attested otherwise in Mesopotamian literature of the first half of the second millennium before Christ—that is, the very period under discussion. This fact is irrefutable evidence of the historicity of both those narratives.

Hagar was one of the Egyptian slaves that Pharaoh gave to Abram back in 12:16. The idea of Abram's begetting children by this younger woman was Sarai's, but when things backfire (v. 4) Sarai lays all the blame on Abram (v. 5). The latter just shrugs his shoulders and tells his wife to handle the matter (v. 6).

The slave Hagar, being an Egyptian, heads south in her flight, though we know from another contemporary document, Hammurabi's Code, that she endangered her life by running away. She travels the many miles from Hebron to Shur, southwest of Beersheba, which was a pretty good distance for a pregnant woman to walk, and there she encounters the "Angel of the Lord" (*malek Adonai*), an expression that appears here for the first time in Holy Scripture (v. 7). The angel's promise to Hagar (vv. 10–12) stands parallel to the promises that Abram himself received in chapters 13 and 15. Although she herself is a slave, the angel tells Hagar that her son will not be.

It is a source of wonderment to this slave that she has been noticed by God (v. 13) in this story of God's concern for the poor, the simple, and the persecuted. Hagar discovers her worth when God sends His angel to care for her. God appears already as the champion of the downtrodden, as He will be especially portrayed in the writings of the Bible's great social prophets.

What should be said about Abram's taking of this slave girl as a sort of second wife? We observe that God did not tell him to do this. It was Sarai's idea. The whole project, that is to say, was of the flesh, not of the Spirit. It is no great thing for a young woman to conceive and bear a child, but a great thing is what God had in mind to do. Sarai's plan was a classic case of man interfering with the plans of God. This was simply a work of the flesh, as St. Paul observed (Galatians 4:21–25).

In this respect, furthermore, the Apostle to the Gentiles saw an allegorical prophecy of the situation of the Jews and Christians with regard to Abraham. The Jews, he argued, were children of Abraham in a fleshly way, unlike Abraham's spiritual paternity of Christians (4:26–28). Christians, not being slaves, are not children of Hagar, whereas the Jews, unfamiliar with freedom in Christ, are still slaves to the flesh and the Law (4:31). *They* are the children of Hagar! This idea closes off a chapter of Galatians that began with the transformation from slavery to freedom (3:29—4:7).

ᔕ Genesis 17 ᔐ

This chapter narrates the circumstances in which Abram and Sarai become Abraham and Sarah (vv. 5, 15).

This second account of God's covenant with Abram is the first instance, of three, intimating the source of the name of his son and heir, Isaac. Isaac was named for laughter, because that name, formed from the verbal root *shq*, literally means "he will laugh." When Abram learns that he, at age 100, and his wife, at age 90, will be the parents of this little boy, what else can he do but laugh (v. 17)?

No one felt the irony of their situation better than Sarah herself, however, who will learn of this divine plan in the next chapter, where she will discover the news while eavesdropping, from within the tent, on a conversation between her husband and the Lord whom he hosted outside. "Sarah your wife shall have a son," she will hear the Latter say. Her response? "Sarah laughed within herself," asserts the Sacred Text, a reaction she will be a tad too quick to disavow when questioned on the matter. "I did not laugh," she will insist. "No," the Lord will press the point, "but you did laugh" (18:9–15).

Later on, right after delivering her son, Sarah will deliver the happy laconism that is the third reference to Isaac's name: "God has made me laugh; all who hear will laugh with me" (21:6). Her own and Abraham's laughter was prompted, of course, by the sheer incongruity of the proposition, because "Abraham and Sarah were old, well advanced in age; and Sarah had passed the age of childbearing" (18:11).

According to the full Christian understanding of the Holy Scriptures, the joy of Abraham and Sarah at the promised birth of Isaac was burdened with prophecy, for his miraculous begetting foretold a later conception more miraculous still. Isaac was, in truth, a type and pledge of "Jesus Christ, the Son of David, the Son of Abraham" (Matthew 1:1). And Mary, mother of this Newer Isaac, having conceived Him in virginity just days before, made perfect her responding song of praise by remembering the mercy that God "spoke to our fathers, to Abraham and to his seed forever" (Luke 1:55).

Did not Abraham himself anticipate with joy the later coming of that more distant Seed? Surely so, for even our Newer Isaac proclaimed, "Your father Abraham rejoiced to see My day, and he saw *it* and was glad" (John 8:56). Like Moses (5:46), Isaiah (12:41), and David (Matthew 22:43), Abraham was gifted to behold, in mystic vision, the final fulfillment of that primeval word, "But My covenant I will establish with Isaac" (Genesis 17:21).

In the second century, St. Irenaeus of Lyons expressed thus the mystery inherent in the figure of Isaac:

Abraham, knowing the Father through the Word, who made heaven and earth, confessed Him as God, and taught by a vision that the Son of God would become a Man among men, by whose arrival his seed would be as the stars of heaven, he longed to see that day, so that he too might embrace Christ, as it were; and beholding Him in the Spirit of prophecy, he rejoiced. (*Against the Heresies* 4.7.1)

ᴄ: GENESIS 18 ᴄ

Two scenes fill this chapter. The first is Abraham's reception of the Lord in the guise of "three men," whom the Christian Church has always pictured as three angels. These Three were either the prophetic prefiguration or the appearance of the Persons of the Holy Trinity in human/angelic form, according to the earliest Christian readings of the text. Because the prophetic promise given about Isaac in this chapter is definitively fulfilled only in the New Testament, it was appropriate that on that occasion God should appear as that Trinity of distinct Persons which the New Testament proclaims Him to be.

St. Ambrose of Milan thus commented on this scene in the second half of the fourth century:

> Prepared to receive strangers, faithful to God, dedicated to ministering and prompt in His service, Abraham beheld the Trinity in a type. He supplemented hospitality with religious fealty, when beholding the Three he worshipped the One, and preserving the distinction of the Persons, he addressed One Lord, offering to Three the honor of his gift, while acknowledging but a single Power. It was not learning that spoke in him but grace, and although he had not learned, he believed in a way superior to us who have learned. Since no one had distorted the representation of the truth, he sees the Three but worships the Unity. He offers three measures of fine meal while slaying but one victim, considering that a single sacrifice is sufficient but a triple gift; a single victim, but a threefold offering. (*Faith in the Resurrection* 2.96)

The second scene in this chapter portrays Abraham's supplication on behalf of Sodom, the city where Lot resides. Knowing that the Lord is prepared to destroy that city for its wickedness, and fearing for the welfare of his nephew and his family, Abraham bravely endeavors to arrange a deal with the Lord, in hopes of having the city spared. In one of the most colorful scenes in a very colorful book, Abraham plays the part of the Bedouin trader, a type commonly met in the Middle East, attempting to arrange a lower price by the process of haggling. Particularly good in this art, Abraham works from a "price" of fifty just men down to a mere ten. He thus serves as the very model of fervent intercessory prayer, unafraid of pressing a point with God. Alas, Abraham knows that there are not even ten just men left in Sodom. Before he can suggest a lower figure, however, the Lord abruptly breaks off the negotiations and departs (v. 33). Sodom is doomed.

ᴄ: GENESIS 19 :ᴐ

To the fine example of hospitality shown by Abraham and Sarah in the previous chapter we now find opposed the terrible example of hospitality shown by the residents of Sodom. Although their failure in the matter of hospitality may not have been the worst of their sins, it was sufficiently serious for Jesus to speak of it in the context of the hospitality that He expected His own apostles to receive when they entered a town (Matthew 10:11–15).

Throughout Holy Scripture, Sodom will be remembered as a very bad place that got exactly what it deserved (Deuteronomy 29:23; Isaiah 13:19; Jeremiah 49:17–18; 50:40; Ezekiel 16:46–48, 55–56; Matthew 11:23–24; Revelation 11:8).

There are striking similarities between Psalm 11(10) and this chapter's description of the overthrow of Sodom. Consider the psalm: "He shall rain down snares upon sinners; / Fire and brimstone and a raging wind shall be the portion of their cup." And Genesis: "Then the Lord rained brimstone and fire on Sodom and Gomorrah from the Lord out of heaven." Or, again, in the psalm: "In the Lord I trust. How will you say to my soul, / 'Flee to the mountains like a sparrow'?" And the angels say to Lot in Genesis: "Escape for your life! Do not look behind you nor stay anywhere in the plain. Escape to the mountains, lest you be overtaken." To which Lot answers: "I cannot escape to the mountains, lest some evil overtake me and I die." And yet again in the psalm: "The righteous Lord loves righteousness; / His face beholds the upright."

But according to the apostle Peter, this explains precisely what transpired in the present chapter of Genesis, where God, "turning the cities of Sodom and Gomorrah into ashes, condemned *them* to destruction, making *them* an example to those who afterward would live ungodly; and delivered righteous Lot, *who was* oppressed by the filthy conduct of the wicked (for that righteous man, dwelling among them, tormented *his* righteous soul from day to day by seeing and hearing *their* lawless deeds)" (2 Peter 2:6–8). And the psalm once more: "The Lord is in His holy temple; / The Lord, His throne is in heaven; / His eyes are fixed upon the poor man, / His eyelids examine the sons of men. / The Lord examines the righteous and the ungodly, / And he who loves unrighteousness hates his own soul." And once again Peter, commenting on the present chapter of Genesis: "*the* Lord knows how to deliver the godly out of temptations and to reserve the unjust under punishment for the day of judgment" (2:9).

Similarly, when Jesus would tell us of the final and catastrophic times, it is to Sodom that He sends us: "Likewise as it was also in the days of Lot: They ate, they drank, they bought, they sold, they planted, they built; but on the day that Lot went out of Sodom it rained fire and brimstone from heaven and destroyed *them* all. Even so will it be in the day when the Son of Man is revealed" (Luke 17:28–30). Indeed, "even so," for we ourselves yet abide in the cities of the plain, "as Sodom and Gomorrah, and the cities around them in a similar manner to these" (Jude 7).

Excursus:
Lot's Lot

Abraham's nephew Lot was no good judge of neighborhoods. First, there was Sodom. With the whole Promised Land from which to choose, "Lot dwelt in the cities of the plain and pitched his tent even as far as Sodom" (13:12). It was a perfectly awful choice. Hardly had Lot and his family moved in when a group of Bedouin kings came and raided the place, taking the whole bunch of them captive (14:1–12). Were it not for the prompt intervention of Uncle Abraham, that probably would have been the last we heard of Lot (14:13–17).

In addition, Sodom was hardly a salubrious place to live, because "the men of Sodom were exceedingly wicked and sinful before God" (13:13). We know that Lot did not enjoy living there. The Scriptures speak of "righteous Lot, who was oppressed by the filthy conduct of the wicked (for that righteous man, dwelling among them, tormented his righteous soul from day to day by seeing and hearing their lawless deeds)" (2 Peter 2:7, 8).

Why, then, did Lot continue to live in such a vile place? He seems to have been one of those many people who, once they have settled down somewhere, are reluctant to move away, long after the situation has proven itself hopeless. Such souls are excessively fond of the familiar, the sort of folk who imagine all manner of evil that may befall them if they should change neighborhoods. "I cannot escape to the mountains," insisted Lot, "lest some evil overtake me and I die" (19:19). If anyone in Holy Scripture, however, should ever have heeded the warning, "Come out of her, my people, lest you share in her sins, and lest you receive of her plagues" (Revelation 18:4), surely that man was Lot.

Still, Lot stayed put in Sodom, until it was almost too late. That time of crisis that Jesus called "the days of Lot" (Luke 17:28) had well nigh run its course. Loudly sounded, even now, the hour of its overthrow. The brimstone was ready, with the pitch pots boiling to the brim, and the rescuing angels were urging Lot to hurry: "Arise, take your wife and the two daughters you have, and get out, lest you be destroyed with the transgressions of the city. . . . Escape for your life! . . . Escape to the mountains, lest you be overtaken" (Genesis 19:15, 17).

Second, there was Zoar. Even as he fled from Sodom, Lot already began to miss the old neighborhood and was reluctant to move too far away. When the angels pressed him to flee to the mountains, he begged them for a compromise. How about Zoar, little Zoar, not far from Sodom? "See now," Lot pleaded pathetically, "this city, which is small, is near enough to flee to for refuge, and I shall escape there (is it not a little one?) and my soul shall live" (19:20).

So Lot moved to Zoar, and his soul did live, but not his wife's, alas. Zoar was simply too proximate to Sodom, and it was not safe for Lot's family to remain so immediate to the scene of the overthrow. His wife succumbed to the temptation to look back, in spite of the angelic admonition not to do so (19:17, 26). Her backward glance to Sodom became, for all time, the symbol of those unwilling to put sufficient distance between themselves and sin. Her punishment stands forever as a portent to God's people: "Remember Lot's wife" (Luke 17:32).

In spite of the unflattering picture of him in these biblical stories, Lot is remembered in the Bible as a righteous man. As we have seen, the apostle Peter uses the word "righteous" three times in the two verses he devotes to Lot. In this respect Peter followed the example of the Wisdom of Solomon, which spoke thus of Lot:

> Wisdom rescued a righteous man
> When the ungodly were perishing,
> For he escaped the fire that descended on
> the five cities,
> Concerning which a testimony still remains:

A barren land continually blackened with
    smoke,
Trees bearing fruit which does not ripen
    in season,
And a pillar of salt standing as a
    monument
To an unbelieving soul. (10:6–7)

One observes that when the Bible calls Lot
righteous, the term is somewhat relative; that is, he
is called righteous by way of contrast with those
around him, whether his wife or the citizens of
Sodom. It is largely in this contrast that Lot is held
forth as a model. In the words of St. John of Mount
Sinai, "So we had better imitate Lot, and certainly
not his wife" (Ladder of Divine Ascent 3).

Excursus:
Sodom & Egypt

We have already considered some of the ways in
which Genesis prepares the reader for Exodus. In
the destruction of Sodom we find another such
preparation.

For three and a half days the slain bodies of
God's two faithful witnesses will lie unburied, we are
told, "in the street of the great city which spiritually
is called Sodom and Egypt, where also our Lord was
crucified" (Revelation 11:8–9). The biblical prophets wrote of Sodom (Isaiah 1:10; 3:9) and Egypt
(Ezekiel 23:3, 8, 19, 27) as metaphors for rebellious
societies.

In fact, several striking features of correspondence connect the ancient stories of Sodom and
Egypt in Genesis and Exodus. First, both accounts
portray the deliverance of the just from the midst

of the unjust; Lot's family is saved from Sodom, the Israelites from Egypt. Second, each narrative includes the violent loss of life among the respective inhabitants; fire and brimstone descend on the Sodomites, and the tenth plague is inflicted on the Egyptians, followed by the destruction of Pharaoh's army at the Red Sea. Third, the citizens of both places are punished for oppressing those who sojourned among them; the two angels were menaced in Sodom, and the Israelites were oppressed in Egypt. Fourth, Sodom and Egypt are both punished by cataclysmic forces of nature, whether by the fiery overthrow of the first or the several natural calamities befalling the other. Lastly, just before their ultimate destruction the sinful inhabitants of both Sodom and Egypt are overwhelmed with consummate darkness. This final correspondence, I submit, deserves further comment.

With respect to the menacing Sodomites, the Sacred Text says that the two angels "struck the men who were at the doorway of the house with blindness, both small and great, so that they became weary trying to find the door" (19:11). This darkness of the sinners at Sodom is their penultimate punishment, immediately preceding their destruction. Apparently their blindness lasts to the end. We picture them still groping blindly in the dark when the pitch and brimstone begin to fall.

In the corresponding text in Exodus, the thick darkness of the ninth plague descended on the Egyptians, so that "no one saw his brother for three days; nor did anyone rise from his bed for three days" (Exodus 10:23). Whereas in some of the previous eight plagues of Egypt, Moses had attended to the pleas of Pharaoh and removed the affliction by his prayer to the Lord (8:13, 31; 9:33; 10:19), it does not happen this time. As far as we may discern from the

Sacred Text, this pervading darkness of Egypt, which immediately precedes the slaying of the firstborn sons, endures until Israel's departure.

The striking correspondence between these two stories in Genesis and Exodus was observed a long time ago. Indeed, already in the first century before Christ, the anonymous author of the Wisdom of Solomon compared both the offenses and the punishments of Sodom and Egypt.

With respect to their offenses, the author of Wisdom observes, the Egyptians were guiltier than the Sodomites. In Sodom, after all, the menace had been directed against total strangers, whereas the Egyptians oppressed their "friends," who had lived among them for a long time and had shared their common life and laws (19:13–16).

With respect to punishments, the author of Wisdom describes the Sodomites stricken and sur-rounded with "horrible great darkness" (or "blind-ness," OSB) endeavoring to find their way home from "the doors of the righteous man" Lot (19:17). The darkness over Egypt, however, was worse and lasted three times as long. During this time the Egyptians were shut up in their houses, harassed with fear, exiled from God's "eternal providence," unable to remember anything except the torments of their guilt (17:2–3). Because this darkness was internal, no fire could pierce it, nor were the lights of heaven able to dispel it (17:5). On the contrary, the darkness of Egypt seemed to come from another and mysterious sort of fire (17:6). Because of Egypt's long addiction to the dark arts (17:7), it was now tormented with a profound darkening of the mind, which included the loss of reason (17:8–12).

The darkness chosen by Sodom and Egypt was, in a sense, that original, chaotic darkness "on the face of the deep," antecedent to God's summoning of the

> light. It was the shadow of irreversible damnation.
> This is why the two cities are once again joined in
> the Book of Revelation.

❦ Genesis 20 ❧

This chapter sounds rather similar to the story in chapter 12, where we also learned of the beauty of Sarah and the disposition of men to look upon her with a measure of "coveting." In the present instance, we may bear in mind, Sarah is almost ninety years old and pregnant. This fact says a great deal either of Sarah's beauty or of Abimelech's preferences in women.

We already learned a great deal about Abraham's powers of *persuasion* when he turned to God in prayer. This was hardly surprising, because the Scriptures call him "the friend of God" (2 Chronicles 20:7; Isaiah 41:8; Daniel 3:35 [LXX]; Judith 8:22 [Vulgate]; James 2:23), and God, like the rest of us in this respect, delights in doing favors for His friends. As God's friend, Abraham was blessed with what the Bible calls *parresia*, confidence or even boldness (Ephesians 3:12; Hebrews 4:16), in his approach to the Lord on matters of concern. Like the stalwart widow in the Gospel parable on this subject (Luke 18:1–8), Abraham could be rather persistent, perhaps a tad nagging, when he brought some point of concern to the attention of the Almighty. Accustomed to that mercantile dickering ever common in the Middle East, Abraham knew how to chaffer his way to a bargain, and he incorporated this skill too into his prayer, as it were. We saw this power of his intercessory prayer in Genesis 18:16–33.

Thus in the present chapter, even after God declared to Abimelech, "Indeed, you are a dead man," He went on to promise that Abraham "will pray for you, and you shall live" (vv. 3, 7). And, indeed, "Abraham prayed to God, and God healed Abimelech" (v. 17).

❦ Genesis 21 ❧

We come now to the long-awaited birth of Isaac, concerning which the New Testament says, "By faith Sarah herself also received strength to conceive seed, and she bore a child when she was past the age, because she judged Him faithful who had promised. Therefore from one man, and him as good as dead, were born *as many* as the stars in the sky in multitude—innumerable as the sand which is by the seashore" (Hebrews 11:11–12). While the author of Hebrews praises the faith of Sarah in this respect, the apostle Paul tends rather to stress the faith of Abraham (Romans 4:19–22). The circumcision of Isaac (v. 4), commanded in Genesis 17:9–14, would be explicitly mentioned by St. Stephen in Acts 7:8.

In chapter 16 we already learned that all was not well between Sarah and Hagar after Ishmael was born. At that time, however, Hagar enjoyed the advantage that she had borne a son, and Sarah had not. In the present chapter, that advantage is a thing of the past, and we are not surprised to see that now Hagar and Ishmael are regarded as the mere slaves they are. Ishmael is accused of "scoffing" (NKJV) at the younger child Isaac, perhaps a reference to the kinds of teasing that younger children have been known to suffer from older children. Indeed, one may reasonably speculate that Ishmael had heard disparaging remarks about Sarah and Isaac from his own mother and was simply acting them out. At the very least, Sarah does not want her son playing with a mere slave boy.

So Hagar must go. Ishmael's true situation is revealed in the fact that he is not even named; he is simply "the son of this maidservant" (v. 10). In Sarah's eyes he has become a nonentity. Abraham is faced with a new problem, therefore. Although Ishmael is not Sarah's son except in a purely legal sense that no longer bears legal significance, the older boy is still Abraham's son, and Abraham loves him.

Whatever Sarah's reasons for expelling Hagar and Ishmael, God had His own reasons, and He permitted Sarah's plans to succeed in order for His own reasons to succeed. This is true rather often; God permits evil to prevail for the sake of a greater good that only He can see and plan for. Had Hagar and Ishmael stayed on in Abraham's household, they would have remained slaves. By their departure Ishmael was able to become the father of a great people on the earth (v. 13), a great people with us to this day, the great people of Arabia, for whom God manifested a special providential interest in this text. We will meet this theme of divine providence abundantly in the Joseph story toward the end of Genesis.

The biblical text tends to lose track of Hagar and Ishmael once they arrive in the Negev Desert. The legends of the Arabs tell their own story of how far the mother and child reached in their journey, namely, Mecca. The spring in vv. 14–19 the Arabs identify as the spring of Zamzam, found near the Ka'ba at Mecca, which spring allowed human life to flourish in that place. Thus, Ishmael is credited with the founding of Mecca, which is a religious shrine vastly older than Islam. Thus, according to the Bible, the Arabs too are a great nation, close relatives of the Jews and regarded as their rather bellicose cousins (16:11–12). Indeed, much of the later history of the Fertile Crescent and the Mediterranean Basin was dominated by a single idea: how to restrain the ancient and native bellicosity of Arabia.

~: GENESIS 22 :~

We come now to Abraham's greatest trial of faith. Indeed, the reader is informed, right from the beginning of this story, that Abraham is being tried (v. 1). In this respect there is a great similarity here with the entire premise of the Book of Job, where the reader, but not Job, is instructed that a trial is taking place. In the case of Abraham, this notice to the reader is absolutely essential, because the Jew and the Christian both know that the God of the Bible hates human sacrifice. A trial of faith, on the other hand, is exactly what we should expect from the God of the Bible (cf. 1 Peter 1:6–7).

In the preceding chapter God had promised that Abraham's true posterity would come through Isaac (Genesis 21:12), but now Abraham is commanded to offer up his "beloved son" as a holocaust (v. 2). His obedience is immediate. Abraham, as we have seen, is not the least bit bashful about speaking his mind to God. On the other hand, when he receives from God a direct order, his obedience is invariably prompt and unquestioning (cf. 12:1–4). It is the same here. The trial of faith always has to do with obedience (cf. James 2:20–24).

The two of them, father and son, climb the mountain of sacrifice (v. 6). Since Melito of Sardis in the mid-second century, Isaac's carrying of the wood has always signified to Christians the willingness of God's own Son to take up the wood of the Cross and carry it to the place of sacrifice. In the enigmatic conversation between the two climbers (vv. 7–8), we observe the rich mystery inherent in Abraham's reply that God Himself would provide the victim for the sacrifice; truly He would!

Isaac himself says nothing in reply (vv. 9–10). He is entirely silent. He is like a sheep led to the slaughter that opens not his mouth. Although the concentration of the story is directed at Abraham, we must not lose sight of Isaac, who prefigures the mystery of our redemption. The *substitute* for Isaac, the ram caught by its horns, prefigures the paschal lamb of the Mosaic Covenant, who would be slaughtered in place of Israel's firstborn sons on the night of the Exodus. We are dealing here in chapter 22, then, with the Bible's earliest configuration of the mystery of the substitutionary sacrifice, which is one of the most important categories in the biblical theology of our redemption.

According to Hebrews 11:17–19, Abraham's willingness to offer Isaac displayed his faith in the resurrection. In receiving his son back again, moreover, he enacted a "parable" of the future. (By translating *en parabole* as "in a figurative sense," the NKJV distorts the intent of this text. Abraham did not receive Isaac back in a figurative sense, but in a literal sense.) The "parable" of the event indicates its *pre*figurative sense, in which God Himself received back (alive!) His only Son, whom He had handed over in sacrifice for our salvation.

Excursus:

Isaac, the Paschal Lamb, and Jesus

When the author of Chronicles wrote, "Now Solomon began to build the house of the Lord at Jerusalem on Mount Moriah" (2 Chronicles 3:1), he inserted the theology of Genesis squarely into his account of Israel's sacrificial worship. In fact, this text in Chronicles is the only place in Holy Scripture where the site of the temple is identified as Mount Moriah, the place where Abraham took Isaac to be sacrificed (Genesis 22:2). This is no incidental detail. By introducing this connection of the temple to that distant event, not only does the Chronicler subtly indicate the new temple's continuity with the distant patriarchal period, he also provides his readers with a very rich theme of soteriology.

In fact, chapter 22 is the Bible's first instance of a "substitution" made in the matter of sacrifice. This ram caught in the bush becomes the substitute for Isaac, thus foreshadowing the paschal lamb of the Mosaic Covenant, which would be slaughtered on behalf of Israel's firstborn sons on the night of the Exodus. In chapter 22, then, we are dealing with the Bible's earliest configuration of a category important in biblical soteriology. The paschal lambs, offered in Solomon's temple over the centuries, were all prefigured by that earlier event on Mount Moriah.

The apostle Paul appealed to this category when he wrote that God "did not spare His own Son, but delivered Him up for us all" (Romans 8:32). Echoing this text from Romans, Irenaeus of Lyons wrote, "Abraham, according to his faith, adhered to the command of God's Word, and with a ready mind delivered up, as a sacrifice to God, his only-begotten and beloved son, in order that God also might be pleased to offer up, for all his seed, His own beloved and only-begotten Son, as a sacrifice for our redemption" (Against the Heresies 4.5.4).

If Isaac was a prefiguration of the paschal lambs sacrificed in the Old Testament temple, then he is certainly a prefiguration of the One of whom St. Paul wrote, "Christ, our Passover, was sacrificed for us" (1 Corinthians 5:7). This theme of Christ as the Paschal Lamb has been much developed in the thought and imagery of Holy Church, and this from earliest times. Thus, in the second century St. Justin Martyr wrote, "And the blood of the Passover, sprinkled on each man's door-posts and lintel, delivered those who were saved in Egypt, when the first-born of the Egyptians were destroyed. For the Passover was Christ, who was afterwards sacrificed, as also Isaiah said, 'He was led as a sheep to the slaughter.' And it is written, that on the day of the Passover you seized Him, and that also during the Passover you crucified Him. And as the blood of the Passover saved those who were in Egypt, so also the blood of Christ will deliver from death those who have believed" (*Dialogue with Trypho* III). Such testimonies are ubiquitous in Christian literature.

❦ GENESIS 23 ❧

We come now to the death and burial of Sarah. In a rather gentlemanly fashion, Holy Scripture is generally reluctant to give women's ages (Luke 2:36–37 being an exception), but here we are told that Sarah was 127 years old when she died (thus making Isaac 37 years old at the time). This is the first death mentioned in the family since Abraham began his travels.

Sarah's burial in chapter 23 merits more attention, let me suggest, than it generally gains.

The relative neglect of this story is easy to understand. Less dramatic than the sacrifice of Isaac, which comes right before it, the narrative about Sarah is also less romantic than the wooing of Rebekah, which immediately follows it. To the former it is no match as drama, because the quiet death of an old person is less exciting than the threatened death of a young person. And though Abraham's burial of Sarah is hardly without romance, the tone of this romance is subdued, subtle, more nuanced than the younger love of Isaac and Rebekah. By these criteria, then, Sarah's interment represents a pause, as it were, a respite or slowing down in the Abraham saga. For these reasons it may not especially stand out in the memory of Bible-readers.

Let me also suggest two reasons why the story of Sarah's death and burial deserves more explicit attention. First, the story offers an intriguing psychological portrait of Abraham. Second, it sews a significant theological stitch in the Bible's narrative pattern.

Let us begin with the story's psychological interest in Abraham. A useful way to approach this subject, I think, is by contrasting the figure of Abraham in this account with that in chapter 18. This comparison is amply warranted, inasmuch as both narratives describe Abraham engaged in a "negotiation."

In the earlier story, when Abraham learns of the Lord's plan to destroy Sodom, he fears for the fate of his nephew Lot, a resident of the city. With an enviable but bewildering optimism he endeavors to change the Lord's mind, engaging Him in what is arguably the boldest enterprise of "haggling" ever recorded. No attentive reader will forget how Abraham resolutely lowers the original price, as it were, arguing the sum of required just men from fifty down to ten. The bargaining ends only when the Lord Himself, as though desperate of winning the arbitration, suddenly breaks it off!

In chapter 23 all is different. After Abraham has lain prostrate for a while before the dead body of his wife, he rises, sobered by sorrow, and approaches a local Hittite chieftain in order to obtain a piece of land wherein to bury the cherished companion of his long life. He describes himself now as "a sojourner and a stranger," designations rendered doubly significant in the context of death. Abraham is solemn and deferential. There is no haggling now. His whole demeanor is one of gravity and respect. Sarah is gone. What else matters?

Finally, for a small field containing a cave Abraham pays the exorbitant price of four hundred shekels of silver. (In 3 Kingdoms 16:24 Omri pays only six thousand shekels ["two talents," OSB] of silver for the entire site of the large city of Samaria.) A gentleman does not haggle over the price of his wife's tomb. After such a loss, nothing else is worth much. The old man treads slowly out to the cave, bearing Sarah's body and a lifetime of intimate love.

Second, the story of Sarah's burial in chapter 23 advances the theological theme of Israel's taking possession of the Promised Land. Up to this point in the biblical history, let us recall, Abraham owned no property in Canaan, "not even *enough* to set his foot on" (Acts 7:5). With the purchase of the burial cave of Machpelah, however, his family actually acquires its first piece of real estate in the Holy

Land. This portion of ground becomes the initial installment of Israel's inheritance, the germinal redemption of God's earlier pledge, "I will give this land to your seed" (Genesis 15:18).

In this burial ground an intergenerational transmission of ownership is now established, a "tradition," a "handing on," of Israel's historical identity. The aged flesh of Sarah is but the first deposit the Chosen People adds to the soil of Canaan. Abraham will presently join her at Machpelah, and in due course Isaac and Rebekah, Jacob and Leah too, will lie down in the tombs beside them. Here the ancestors of the Chosen People will return—"dust to dust"—to the earth from which they were taken.

The grave is the place, after all, where time is fixed, durably fused with space. The complex, shadowing mists of the past are coupled forever to the plain but sturdy permanence of the soil. Everything is settled. In the graveyard, history and geography become one.

After Sarah, Abraham would be buried in the same place, along with his son, his grandson, and their wives; all of them rest at Hebron still, awaiting the return of that One who, for a very short while, lay in the grave of the Arimathean.

PART FOUR
THE ISAAC CYCLE

❦

ᗒ GENESIS 24 ᗕ

The doctrine of divine providence is asserted in the biblical thesis that "all things work together for good to those who love God" (Romans 8:28). This "working together" of historical events under divine governance for particular and interrelated purposes is a mystery, of course, but a mystery in two senses.

First, divine providence is a mystery in the sense that it is humanly inscrutable, exceeding even the furthest reaches of our thought, and is known only by faith. That is to say, it pertains to divine revelation. It is not the general, natural *pronoia* of the Stoics and Middle Platonists, but a special providence revealed by God's particular interventions in the structure of history. For this reason Holy Scripture never attempts to explain it. Although the Bible affirms divine providence, it teaches no theory of the matter.

Second, divine providence is also a mystery in the sense that we are initiated into it. It is rendered accessible, that is, to our revelatory experience of it, the discernment of which is a gift of the Holy Spirit. It is particular and personal, sensed through the coherent structure of events. For this reason Holy Scripture not only affirms divine providence, but also portrays the mystery of it through narratives about events.

The story of Joseph, which we shall study presently, is perhaps the most elaborate example of such a narrative. We do not discern *how*, in the Joseph story, "all things *work together* for good to those who love God," but the narrative enables us to perceive it intuitively, buried deep in the events of Joseph's life and conferring coherence on that life. At the end of the story we are able to say, with Joseph, "So now, it was not you who sent me here, but God" (45:8).

In some cases, we can sense God's providential purpose in a biblical story by the insinuated dynamics of the story itself, without our attention being drawn to it by any explicit statement. Examples of this are found in the Book of Ruth and, with far greater subtlety, the Book of Esther. In the latter story, in fact, God's intrusive activity in the events is so subtle that He is not even mentioned!

In other instances the Bible conveys the providential nature of a story by the direct insertion of it through the voice of the narrator. Through such an insertion, the story takes on an entirely different flavor, being transfigured, so to speak, from secular to sacred. For instance, the tale of David's escape from Saul at Hachilah (1 Kingdoms 26) is transformed into an account of divine providence by the plain statement that "all were sleeping, because a deep sleep from the Lord fell upon them" (26:12). Similarly the biblical narrator says, in the context of Absalom's revolt, that "the Lord had purposed to defeat the good advice of Ahithophel, to the intent that the LORD might bring disaster on Absalom" (2 Samuel 17:14, NKJV).

Another literary method of conveying God's providential purpose in a biblical story is to place the affirmation of it in the mouth of one of the characters. As I have mentioned, this is the method followed in the Joseph story, in the scene where he reveals himself to his brothers (45:5–7; 50:15–20).

This style also characterizes the present story of the wooing of Rebekah. In this exquisitely crafted account of God's historical intervention in response to prayer, two features should especially be noted.

First, the story is told twice, initially by the narrator (vv. 1–26) and then a second time by a character within the narrative, namely the servant (vv. 34–48). This deliberate doubling of the story, which obliges the reader to think about its implications a second time, also serves the purpose of placing the theme of divine providence more completely within the fabric of the tale. In the first telling, the reader is struck by how quickly the servant's prayer is heard—"it happened, before he finished speaking" (v. 15). This promptness of God's response is emphasized in the second telling—"before I finished speaking in my mind" (v. 45). God is encountered in the servant's experience of the event that comes crashing in, as it were, on his prayer.

Second, the doubling of the narrative is not artificial. It is essential, rather, to the motive of Rebekah and her family in their decision that she should accompany the servant back to Abraham's home and become the wife of Isaac. That is to say, the characters themselves are made aware that God has *spoken* through the narrated events. *They* perceive God's providence: "The command [*dabar*] comes from the Lord; we cannot speak [*dabber*] to you either good or bad. Here is Rebekah before you; take her and go, and let her be your lord's son's wife, as the Lord has spoken [*dibber*]" (vv. 50–51). The event itself was a "word" from God, a *dabar*. That is to say, given the servant's testimony, it was clear that all things had worked together "for good to those who love God."

❧ GENESIS 25 ❧

Abraham, having spent most of his life childless, seems to have overdone it a bit toward the end. He married a woman named Keturah, who bore him quite a family (vv. 1–6). This brief account sits somewhat outside of the central core of the biblical narrative, almost as an afterthought. Although it may have taken place prior to the marriage of Isaac in the previous chapter, the story is told at the very end, just before Abraham's death. Its insertion into the Bible manifests a concern to show that the Israelites were related by blood to other peoples who lived in the region, particularly the Midianites and Kedemites ("Easterners"), nomadic tribes of the Arabian and Syrian deserts.

At the same time, however, care is taken to show that Abraham kept this later family separate from Isaac (v. 6), who alone was the heir of the divine promises.

At Abraham's death, he is buried in the same plot that he purchased earlier at Hebron for the burial of Sarah. Ishmael and Isaac join to bury their father, a fact apparently indicating that some contact between the two households had been maintained (vv. 7–11). The scene of Abraham's burial, uniting these two peoples of the Middle East, seems especially poignant in our own day.

Now that Abraham has died, the Bible's interest will go to the history of Isaac and his family. This is not done, however, until the author has tidied up Ishmael and his own progeny (vv. 12–18). Here we observe that twelve tribes trace their lineage back to Ishmael, a parallel to the twelve tribes that will spring from the seed of Jacob later on. Various of these Arabian tribes will be mentioned again in Holy Scripture, in Exodus and Chronicles for example.

The latter part of this chapter concerns Isaac's own sons, twins who begin to fight even in Rebekah's womb (vv. 22–23). These men were already rivals, and, according to Romans 9:10–13, God had already chosen one of them in preference over the other. Just as God chose Isaac in preference to Ishmael, He chose Jacob in preference to Esau. "Choice" in this context does not pertain to eternal salvation, but to the role that Jacob was destined to play in the history of salvation. God's "rejection" of Esau means only that he was not chosen to play that role; in the same sense, God will "reject" the older brothers in favor of David (1 Kingdoms 16:5–12). There is nothing in the Sacred Text, either in Genesis, Malachi 1:1–5, or Romans, even faintly to suggest that Esau was predestined to hell.

Jacob is obviously the shrewder of the two men (vv. 29–34). Indeed, Esau comes off as a bit of a spiritual klutz, forfeiting his birthright for a single meal. He should serve as a warning to Christians themselves, who may be tempted to squander their own birthright in favor of some immediate satisfaction (cf. Hebrews 12:14–17). The attaining of a birthright requires patience and endurance; it is something to be valued and waited for. In this respect, we learn something of the superior patience of Jacob, which will become even clearer in his dealings with Laban later on.

Excursus:
Jacob & Esau

In the divine choice of Jacob over Esau the apostle Paul saw a paradigm of God's election of the Gentiles when the Jewish people, taken as whole, rejected the messianic identity of Jesus. Several sources in the New Testament addressed this thorny problem in some form. In most of these sources the New Testament writers recognized that Israel's failure, its "falling away," had itself been prophesied in the Old

Testament, chiefly in the Book of Isaiah. This approach to the problem is clearest in John (12:37–41), but we find it in other authors as well (Matthew 13:10–15; Mark 4:10–12; Luke 8:10; Acts 28:23–28).

Paul went further. Israel's failure, he said, was not only prophesied but also providential. God, foreknowing Israel's defection, made use of that defection; He prepared ahead of time to make it serve as the occasion and the impulse for the justification and salvation of the Gentiles. He did this by His mysterious, unfathomable, providential guidance of history. Such is the argument of Romans 9–11.

Although the verb "predestine" does not appear in these chapters (nor is the noun "predestination" to be found anywhere at all in the New Testament), the development of Paul's thought in Romans 9–11, his treatment of the problem of the divine election, surely extends his teaching on predestination in Romans 8. In order not to misunderstand Paul's meaning about divine election, therefore, it is important to consider what Paul says, and does not say, about predestination.

Otherwise we run the risk of regarding Paul's historical illustrations, such as Esau and Pharaoh, as examples of eternal loss. This would be not only an unwarranted inference but also a mammoth distortion of Paul's thought. It may be the case, of course, that both Esau and Pharaoh have been condemned to hell, but there is nothing about this question in the writings of Paul. Esau and Pharaoh serve as examples, rather, of God's mysterious ability, based on His foreknowledge, to bring good out of evil in the course of history.

Thus, the moral obtuseness of Esau, which we have seen in Genesis, and the hardened heart of Pharaoh are predestined, were foreseen and are "arranged ahead of time," to be the occasions of grace for Jacob and Israel, before any of these had been born or had performed any good or evil act (Romans 9:11). Jacob and the Israelites are made vessels of election, recipients and containers of God's blessing, while Esau and Pharaoh become "vessels of wrath prepared for destruction" (Romans 9:22). All of this, says Paul, was predestined, was arranged ahead of time, by God in His wisdom and mercy.

Paul begins his argument in Romans 9 by establishing the principle that mere physical descent does not make someone an Israelite. (He will use the words "Israel" and "Israelite" in this section because his major Old Testament prefiguration is Jacob, whose other name is Israel.) Consequently, the Jews can make no special claims on God merely by the fact that they are Abraham's descendants (Romans 9:6–10).

Even God's election of Israel, after all, was not prompted by any merits on the part of Israel. This is proved by God's promise and mysterious intervention to bring about the conception and birth of Isaac (9:8–10). As we have seen, that predestined intervention was a clear illustration of God's ability to give life to the dead and call to being those things that did not exist (4:17).

Even regarding the descendants of the promised Isaac ("our father"), God distinguished between Jacob and Esau, before either was formed or had made any moral choice (9:11). God's own choice, prior to either man's choice, fell on Jacob. He loved Jacob, that is to say, before Jacob ever loved Him (9:13; 1 John 4:19). God's historical choice of Jacob/Israel prefigured His predestined election of the Gentile Christians, who had done nothing to merit God's favor (9:12). This biblical example, Paul contends, foreshadowed the present situation of the Gentile believers. God had used Esau's defection, which He foreknew, as the occasion to make Jacob His chosen vessel in the history of salvation. He does the same now for the Gentile believers.

As for Esau himself, he got exactly what he deserved. His own place in biblical history was to be shoved off to the side, a vessel of dishonor (9:21). Instead of inheriting the Promised Land, which should have been his birthright, he was obliged to become merely a desert chieftain (Malachi 1:2–3). Contemning his own inheritance, he made that choice himself (Hebrews 12:16).

In other words, Esau's conduct and its results served as an historical foreshadowing of what occurred to the greater part of the Jewish people in Paul's time. They had shunned their true inheritance, which thus passed to the Gentiles. They became the castaways of salvation history, the Christians' elder brothers, shoved off to the side. They could not blame God for this. They themselves, like Esau, had made the choice.

The "hate" of Romans 9:13 ("Esau I have hated") is, of course, a standard hyperbole in Holy Scripture (Luke 14:26). Strictly speaking, God hates nothing that He has made. That understood, the real mystery is not how God could hate Esau. The real mystery is what prompted God to love Jacob. This we do not know, for He has mercy on whom He has mercy, and He shows compassion to whom He shows compassion (Romans 9:15). That is God's business, not ours. We are content to know that God treats no man unjustly. Esau got what he deserved, and Jacob didn't. Our trust, as Christians, is that God will not treat us as we deserve.

God's predestinations, His predetermined adjustments to the unfolding of history, are not arbitrary. They are founded on the divine foreknowledge. "Predetermination is the work of the divine command based on foreknowledge," wrote John of Damascus in the eighth century (*De Fide Orthodoxa* 2.30). God's sovereignty over history, then, is no detriment to man's ability to make moral choices. It is chiefly manifest, rather, in God's ability to bring good results out of man's bad choices. God's sovereignty is in no way challenged by man's decisions.

For this reason, God's election frees no man from his moral obligations. God's ability to bring good out of evil does not warrant anyone to do evil. Nor should it lessen any man's efforts to do good. "Now if men in their choices choose what is best," said John Chrysostom, "much more does God. Moreover, the fact of their being chosen is both a sign of the loving kindness of God and of their own moral goodness. . . . God Himself has rendered us holy, but we must continue to be holy. A holy man is someone who partakes of the faith; a blameless man is someone who leads an irreproachable life" (*Homilies on Ephesians* 1).

The man whom God rejects, therefore, has no just case against God. God causes no man's failure. Even though the Scriptures speak of God's hardening of Pharaoh's heart (Romans 9:17–18; Exodus 4:21; 7:3; 9:12), this is a metaphor describing God's providential use of Pharaoh's hardened heart. Pharaoh himself is the only one responsible for his hard heart (Exodus 7:14, 22; 8:5, 19, 32). Pharaoh's sin cannot be ascribed to God, as though God had decreed that sin. God foreknew that sin and determined ahead of time—predestined—how to employ that sin to bring about His own deliverance of Israel from Egypt. There is no unrighteousness in God (Romans 9:14).

Like Esau's, Pharaoh's role or place in salvation history is negative. It represents a resistance to grace that God employs to show even more grace. The resistance to grace, on the part of Esau and Pharaoh, is providentially subsumed into God's plan of deliverance, being used as the contrary force (the "push backwards") in a process of historical dialectic, much as a man steps on a rock, the friction and resistance from which enable him to go forward. This is what Paul sees happening among the greater part of the Jewish people of his own day. Their resistance to God's mercy has served only to enhance and extend that mercy, for God does nothing except in mercy.

It is fallacious, therefore, to argue that God's ability to bring good out of evil should oblige Him not to blame those who do evil (9:19). Paul had earlier refuted that line of argument (6:1, 15).

To someone who would argue this way, Paul responds, "So who put you in charge of history?" God takes into His hands the raw material of history, "the same lump" (9:21), and shapes it as He wills. He forces no one to be evil; He compels no man to be a vessel of wrath and dishonor, but God does have His uses for vessels of wrath and dishonor. God is the potter of history (Isaiah 14:9; 29:16; 45:9; 64:8; Wisdom 15:7; Sirach 38:39–40; Theophilus of Antioch, *Ad Autolycum* 2:26). He is fashioning His purpose from the common clay of human history. The prophet Jeremiah, far from regarding this image as an excuse for human failure, employs it as a summons to repentance: "Behold, I form calamities and devise a plan against you. Therefore, let each turn away from his way of evil and do good in your practices" (Jeremiah 18:11).

Some vessels are not worth keeping. They are "prepared for destruction" (Romans 9:22), meaning "ready for the dump." After they have served their purpose, they are no longer part of the process of salvation history. Such were Esau and Pharaoh, who serve no other purpose in Holy Scripture than as examples of men who resisted God. Doing evil, they thus served their purpose in God's redemptive interventions of grace, and now they have been tossed out on the ashbin. This lot they brought upon themselves, as is clear in the biblical accounts of them.

The vessels of honor, on the other hand, the "vessels of mercy, which He had prepared beforehand for glory" (9:23), share in the everlasting exaltation that marks God's work of deliverance. These are taken from among Jews and Gentiles (9:24).

❧ GENESIS 26 ❧

God's historical choice is now further narrowed; the promises made to Abraham are now made to Isaac, as they had not been made to Ishmael (vv. 1–5). On the other hand, Isaac is clearly a "transition patriarch," between Abraham and Jacob. There are almost no stories about Isaac, except in relation to either his father or his sons. Whereas both Abraham and Jacob traveled in both Mesopotamia and Egypt, Isaac never leaves the Promised Land.

The story about Rebekah and Abimelech (vv. 6–11) is strikingly similar to two earlier stories about Sarah, and the she-is-my-sister trick is something that Isaac evidently learned from his father. There are differences among the stories, nonetheless. In the present case, we observe that the wife is not actually removed to the other man's house; Abimelech does not go quite so far on the present occasion. He has evidently become just a wee bit more cautious; this time it does not take a divine revelation for him to discover the truth. He simply watches the couple more closely, until one day he sees them engaged in amorous exchanges (we will not speculate) that reveal that they are husband and wife. Indeed, as it turns out, Abimelech himself never admits being interested in Rebekah; he simply explains that he feared somebody else might be!

The "revelation" in this chapter happens differently from those in chapters 12 and 20. In the former two stories, God manifested the truth by a supernatural intervention easily discerned. In the present story God's revelation to Abimelech is subtler; indeed, God is not even mentioned in connection with it. That is to say, God's intervention and deliverance need not be spectacular in order to be real. It is sufficient that "all things work together for good to those who love God" (Romans 8:28).

In the controversy about the wells (vv. 12–22), the word "Philistine" is an anachronism, because the real Philistines, to whom the regions about the Aegean Sea were native, would not arrive on the coast of Canaan for several centuries. The mention of them here is something on the order of saying that "Columbus discovered America." While there may be some disagreement whether or not Columbus actually did so, no one disagrees that the name "America" was not in place when Columbus arrived. Similarly here, the "Philistines" are simply those who lived in the land that would later be inhabited by the Philistines.

In this story, we observe that Isaac has inherited the peace-loving, unassertive disposition of his father. When there is trouble, he defuses it by meekness. And in his case too, the "meek shall inherit the earth."

The account of Isaac's vision (vv. 23–25) links his name to the ancient shrine of Beersheba, much as Abraham's name was associated with Hebron, and Jacob's will be with Shechem and Bethel. The account itself is similar to that in chapter 17.

We recall from chapter 24 that Isaac was not to marry any of the local talent, the idolatrous Hittite girls who lived in the neighborhood. A wife was procured for him, rather, "from the old country." This wife, Rebekah, sharing the family's dislike of these local girls, is understandably less than thrilled by Esau's marrying them (vv. 34–35). She will determine that Jacob, her own favorite son, will be spared such a fate (cf. 27:46). The two final verses of this chapter prepare us for the story in chapter 28.

Excursus:
Abimelech in Love

Abimelech, the king of Gerar, had an appreciative eye for handsome women. True, this trait brought him briefly to grief on one occasion, but they say he learned from the experience.

The incident began when some newcomers, Abraham and Sarah, settled in the neighborhood. When Sarah was introduced as Abraham's sister, poor Abimelech at one glance felt himself going all gooey inside. At the sight of this beautiful, apparently unmarried woman, the king's ardently smitten heart started to flutter like a leaf in the breeze. With a single look at the lady (a look that sober minds may have judged, nonetheless, injudiciously long), Abimelech found his knees shaky and his throat dry. This lovely Sarah was surely meant for him, the king had no doubt.

And, being the king, Abimelech was accustomed to getting what he wanted. Indeed, royal courting and romancing were rather uncomplicated in those days; Abimelech simply sent over to Abraham's place and had Sarah removed to the royal palace. It all happened very fast. In fact, the story so far is contained in just one Bible verse (20:2).

Now in the considerations that follow, let us be temperate with Abimelech. He was, after all, a man in love, and men thus stricken have been known to act precipitously once in a while. Let us be gentle with him.

Nonetheless, let us also be frank. Abimelech should have known that this was not a smart move. Certain features of the case, if he had thought on them, might have prompted the king to a greater and more salutary caution.

Not least among these was the fact that lovely Sarah was ninety years old at the time (17:17), and Abimelech should have given that circumstance the reflection it deserved. This was *not* good. Please understand, no matter how well preserved and retentive of her youth the lady may be, the abrupt abduction of a ninety-year-old woman for amorous purposes is generally considered bad form. Among gentlemen, at least, it simply isn't done. And when it is done, let me tell you, most of the time the thing just doesn't work out.

Second, Abimelech was wrong to take at face value the assertion, "She is my sister." That was one of Abraham's old tricks to avoid getting his throat slit by other men who, it appears, were forever falling in love with his unusually attractive wife. Years before, when he and Sarah were visiting Egypt, the pharaoh down there had been similarly smitten with her. Not only had Abraham on that occasion saved his own life by recourse to his she-is-my-sister routine, but also the pharaoh gave Abraham lots of nice presents to honor him. Then, when the whole thing blew up in the pharaoh's face, Abraham still got to keep the presents (12:11–20). That is to say, the ruse paid off.

Abraham, if questioned further about Sarah's being his sister, could always point out that "sister" in Hebrew really means "female relative," and Sarah was a blood relative—his half-sister, in fact (20:12). Obviously this convenient arrangement was useful for throwing would-be rivals into confusion, nor did Abraham much scruple on the matter. Although we are never told Sarah's views about it, we do know that she tended to appreciate the humor and irony of things (18:11–12).

Anyway, to return to our story, Abimelech thought Sarah definitely the woman of his dreams. These dreams, however, began turning sour right away: "But God came to Abimelech in a dream by night, and said to him, 'Indeed, you are a dead man because of the woman you have taken, for she is a man's wife'" (20:3). Abimelech argued his innocence, a point the Lord conceded, and in the morning Sarah was returned, untouched, to her husband.

Both of them were rebuked for the deception, but Abimelech still loaded them down with more presents (20:4–16).

As I remarked earlier, Abimelech learned from the experience. Some years later Isaac, the son of Abraham and Sarah, came to settle at Gerar with his beautiful wife Rebekah. Once again, sure enough, Isaac tried to pass Rebekah off as his "sister"; she was, in fact, a cousin. This time, however, chary Abimelech did not bite. He simply kept a watchful eye on the couple, until one day he "looked through a window and saw Isaac, showing endearment to Rebekah his wife" (26:8). "Aha, I knew it," thought he to himself, "you just can't be too careful these days."

⌒: GENESIS 27 :⌒

The shrewdness of Rebekah (vv. 1–13) was a family trait, which we have already seen in Jacob's snatching of Esau's birthright. Very shortly we will find Jacob matching wits with Rebekah's brother, Laban. If we are disposed to judge Rebekah's favoritism too harshly, it will be useful to bear in mind that the Lord had already given her a special insight into the matter: "Two nations are in your womb, / And two peoples shall be separated from your body. / One shall be stronger than the other, / And the older shall serve the younger" (25:23). Rebekah knew which son was which, so she knew which son would do the serving and which would be served. If such was God's plan, Rebekah saw no harm in moving things in the right direction, as it were. Moved by a mixture of faith and anxiety, Rebekah decides to take the fulfillment of prophecy into her own hands. (We recall that Sarah also did that, when she gave Hagar to Abraham as a second wife.)

Christians have long been bothered by Rebekah's and Jacob's deception of Isaac. Their discomfort is understandable, but we should bear in mind that Holy Scripture is simply telling us what happened. The cunning of the mother and the mendacity of the son are not being held up for our emulation. Ultimately this is a story about what God does, not man. This is "mystery, not mendacity," said St. Augustine.

There is no indication that anyone but Rebekah had received that revelation of God's plan, so we should not be surprised that Isaac is unaware of it. Thus, his physical blindness becomes a symbol of his inability to see what is going on, according to God's plan. His favoring of Esau over Jacob already puts him outside of God's will; that is to say, his preference between his sons is not that of God. Being outside of God's will, therefore, he is easily deceived. Acting outside of God's will is a sure step toward deception. On at least two levels in this account, therefore, Isaac is acting blindly.

The blessing of the Promised Land, then, goes to Jacob, not to Esau (vv. 26–29). Isaac unwittingly shifts God's promises to his younger son, Jacob, and these promises will, in due course, pass to the latter's descendants (Deuteronomy 7:13–14; 33:28).

The account of Esau's return (vv. 30–33) is especially dramatic. The inspired author is not so preoccupied with the underlying theology as to lose contact with the human and emotional components of this remarkable story. Isaac begins to tremble. At once he becomes aware that he has been acting in ignorance. Yet that blessing, once given, was the instrument of the divine will. He had become the unwitting agent of God's purposes, which were quite distinct from his own. Thus, this is one of the Bible's great stories of those who accomplish God's will in ignorance and even contrary to their own intentions. It is not a story about fate, but it does have some literary similarities to Greek stories about fate. (The story of blind Teiresias, in the *Antigone* of Sophocles, comes to mind.)

Especially poignant are the tears of Esau, thus foiled a second time. It was not that Isaac had only one blessing to give. The really big blessing, however, the blessing that handed on the promises of God, was already taken and was no longer available. Esau, the man who had earlier thought so little of his birthright, was not worthy to receive the blessing of the firstborn, and Holy Scripture shows no great sympathy for him (cf. Hebrews 12:16–17).

Even acting in mistake, Isaac acted "by faith," according to the Epistle to the Hebrews (11:20). Faith is compatible with a great deal of error, blindness, and misunderstanding.

Esau's blessing (vv. 39–40) does give some reprieve to his descendants; they will not serve Jacob's descendants forever. Their subjection will eventually come to an end (cf. 4 Kingdoms 8:20–22; 2 Chronicles 21:8–10).

Excursus:
Esau, the Modern Man

Though his appearance in history was, I suppose, a bit too early to warrant the term, "modern man" seems an apt expression for the biblical character Esau. At least we can call him modern in one large and defining sense: Esau, for the sole purpose of gratifying an immediate impulse, thoughtlessly betrayed an inherited treasure. The New Testament, in its only complaint against him, describes Esau as a "profane person . . . who for one morsel of food sold his birthright" (Hebrews 12:16).

First, Esau's underlying weakness was a lack of elementary self-control. As a rugged outdoorsman (Genesis 25:27), perhaps he thought of himself as a man of tough discipline. Clearly, however, the very opposite was true. Esau was unable to control his appetite even long enough for a meal to be prepared for him. Like a nursing infant, he insisted on being fed Right Now, as though he would otherwise perish: "Look, I am about to die. What good then is this birthright to me?" (25:32). Undisciplined Esau, that is to say, gave up his inheritance for a slight but instant gratification, and this is the first and radical reason I call him a modern man.

Esau was also modern in a second way, in that he had no real sense of the relative worth of things. Because he had cheaply sold something material, he assumed that he could just as cheaply purchase something spiritual. Embracing the principle that man lives by bread alone, he nonetheless fancied that a higher benediction was still available to him, pretty much at the same price. Having lost his birthright for a bowl of soup, he planned to gain his blessing with a plate of venison.

There is a third display of Esau's modernity: He was slow to learn that the future is very much tied to the past. Some blessings—and among them the very best—are inseparable from birthrights, so that the reckless squandering of the one renders unlikely the acquisition of the other. Those, therefore, who contemn the past have little chance for a future. Poor Esau! The New Testament describes his plight: "For you know that afterward, when he wanted to inherit the blessing, he was rejected, for he found no place for repentance, though he sought it diligently with tears" (Hebrews 12:17).

There is a fourth sense in which Esau appears as a modern man—the willful assertion of his individuality at the expense of his personhood. Persons, after all, are defined by their relationships to others, especially others in the past. Indeed, persons receive their very names from those who arrived in this world before them. There is no personhood without community and tradition, because persons are created when someone else, someone older, tells us who we are. Persons, thus, are necessarily formed within the context of an eldership; a person is someone who stands under the authority of what Ken Myers has called "a community of binding address," in which those who go before have authority over those who come after. Personhood, therefore, requires a living tradition and a committed acquiescence in the authority of elders.

An individual is something quite different. His relations to others do not define him. He is, on the contrary, very much self-defined. He is someone "distinct from" others. The Bible required but few words to tell the trait of the individualist: "Thus Esau despised *his* birthright" (25:34, NKJV). An individual is a "self-made man." He does not derive who he is as a free and generous bequest from the past; he acquires it by his independence and self-determination in the present.

In these various ways of describing him as modern, I have in mind chiefly Esau's deliberate alienation from what could and should have been his own, and what he could and should have been able to bequeath to his posterity. His sin consisted in separating himself from tradition, the transmission of an intergenerational inheritance.

The character of Esau goes far to illustrate "post-cultural man," a term coined by Christopher Clausen to identify the deeply isolated individual deprived of the wealth and wisdom of a living heritage. Emancipated from answering to the authority of the past, this post-cultural man is necessarily deprived of a fully human community in the present. He belongs only to the "now," reduced to a spiritually meager, less-than-human cohabitation in what Robert Bellah calls a "life-style enclave." Poor Esau, coming from nowhere, now lives nowhere and has nowhere to go.

PART FIVE
THE JACOB CYCLE

❦

❈ GENESIS 28 ❈

As we saw in the previous chapter, Rebekah does not want Jacob simply to *flee* from the possible vengeance of Esau. She correctly wants Jacob to be sent away by his father. There are several things to be said about Isaac's sending Jacob away (vv. 1–5).

First, there is a sense of historical continuity. Isaac is aware that he is handing on a legacy that he himself received. The current family crisis is not treated simply as a matter of the present; it is subsumed into a larger historical picture.

Second, there is the prayer and promise of fertility. The effects of this prayer (twelve sons and a daughter!) show how powerful a man of prayer Isaac really was (cf. also 25:21).

Third, Jacob continues the tradition of being a "stranger" (v. 4), like his grandfather and father. This theme will be picked up in the New Testament: "By faith [Abraham] dwelt in the land of promise as *in* a foreign country, dwelling in tents with Isaac and Jacob, the heirs with him of the same promise" (Hebrews 11:9).

Esau, having twice failed to please his parents by his choice of wives, decides this time to choose a bride from within the family (vv. 6–9). Alas, he marries into the discredited side of the family! One sometimes has the impression that Esau's brow was branded with the word "Loser."

The religious experience of Jacob at Bethel is divided into two parts: his vision, in which God speaks (vv. 10–15), and his thoughtful reaction *within* the dream (vv. 16–22). This division of religious experience into the visionary and the deliberative is found in other places of Holy Scripture, such as the case of Peter in Acts 10:9–17 and several places in Ezekiel. Jacob's is a night-vision, like that of

Abraham in chapter 15 and Isaac in chapter 26; indeed, God says to him (v. 15) much the same things that He said to Abraham (15:17–18) and to Isaac (26:24–25). Thus, all three of the patriarchs have visions in the night, and all three establish shrines: Abraham at Hebron, Isaac at Beersheba, Jacob at Bethel.

Bethel ("house of God") is the place where earth and heaven are joined, as though by an umbilical cord (v. 12). When Jacob rises in the morning, he consecrates the place, somewhat terrified that he had picked, as his place to sleep, the very spot where heaven and earth are joined; he was nearly run over by all the angelic traffic, as it were.

Bethel is a type and prefigurement, of course, of the real house of God, where heaven and earth are joined, Jesus Christ our Lord (John 1:43–51). Christians since the second century have regarded Jacob's ladder as the ladder of Christ. For this reason, Jacob poured oil (*chrisma*) on the stone, making it a "*Christ*ian stone" (cf. Justin Martyr, *Dialogue with Trypho* 86).

❧ GENESIS 29 ❧

At about noon (v. 7) Jacob arrives at the city well of Haran, where he finds three shepherds that have already assembled with their flocks (v. 2). They are waiting for other shepherds to arrive, so that there will be enough manpower to remove the very heavy stone that covers the mouth of the well (vv. 3, 8). It says a great deal of Jacob's physical strength that he is able, all by himself, to do the job (v. 10). (And we recall that he was the weaker of the twins borne by Rebekah!)

Just as Jacob begins to inquire about Laban, his mother's brother, his interlocutors point out to him that Laban's daughter, Rachel, is approaching. Thus, like Abraham's servant in chapter 24, Jacob is promptly blessed by the arrival of a young woman who proves to be a lady of destiny (vv. 6, 9–12). Once again like the servant in the earlier case, Jacob tells the whole story, "all that happened," to Laban (v. 13).

(It is useful to note that Laban calls Jacob "my brother," whereas Jacob is really his nephew. The reader should bear in mind that the words "brother and sister," when used in Holy Scripture, only rarely mean what we ourselves intend when we employ those same words today. The reason for this is very simple: the Semitic biblical languages, Hebrew and Aramaic, have no other way to designate relatives in general, and this Semitic usage has spilled over into the Greek parts of the Bible as well. "Brothers and sisters" is simply the common way of designating relatives in Holy Scripture and throughout the languages of the Middle East. Most of the time in the Bible, then, the expression "brothers and sisters" designates simply "male and female relatives." Whenever, therefore, these expressions appear in Holy Scripture, they should be understood only in the general sense of "relative," unless the context indicates otherwise. There are earlier instances of this idiomatic usage in Genesis, such as 13:8. Twice more Abraham's nephew, Lot, would be called Abraham's brother [14:14, 16]. Other biblical examples abound. This usage is commonly known among historians and linguists, but modern readers tend to forget it when they come across the "brothers and sisters" of Jesus in the Gospels. Contemporary readers need to remember that the entire Christian tradition without exception was aware of this idiomatic usage, including all the Fathers of the Church, both East and West, all the medieval theologians, and all the major Protestant Reformers, such as Luther, Calvin, and Zwingli; all these writers, consequently, explicitly denied that Jesus had any physical brothers and sisters born of the same mother.)

Immediately Jacob falls in love with Rachel, whose physical appearance is contrasted with that of her older sister, Leah (vv. 13–30). Jacob's preference is clear, and he agrees to work the seven years that his cunning uncle requires. For Laban, however, Jacob's preference in the matter posed a bit of a problem. While there would be no difficulty finding a husband for Rachel, Laban was less certain about Leah's prospects. During those seven years, no one had sought the hand of Leah. (The medieval Jewish commentator Rashi speculated that Leah was afraid that, if Jacob married her younger sister, she herself would have to marry the older brother Esau, and she wanted nothing of that!)

Laban determined, therefore, to look out for the fortunes of his elder daughter. Accordingly Laban pulls a rather mean trick, a trick rendered possible because the bride was veiled (vv. 21–25). It is not hard to figure out the wily Laban, who does not shrink from taking advantage when he can. He studies situations carefully, spots weaknesses in his associates, and consistently uses people. There is a special irony in the account, as well. Jacob deceived his father in chapter 27; now he is in turn deceived by his new father-in-law; in each case it was a matter of a "false identity."

Laban then makes the "magnanimous gesture" of offering Jacob both daughters as wives (v. 27), which procures the wives' father, of course, another seven years of service from Jacob. (This sororite marriage will later be forbidden in the Mosaic Law; cf. Leviticus 18:18.)

Laban has clearly thought this whole plan out ahead of time. This procedure is Laban's way of keeping his property in the family. He has now procured this apparently dimwitted nephew, an energetic worker who will do whatever is required of him. This nephew will be married to both of his daughters. All of their children will be Laban's; all the property will be his; everything will be his (31:43). From this point on, the story becomes a rivalry of wits between Jacob and Laban. Jacob will prove more than a match for his father-in-law.

❃ GENESIS 30 ❧

This chapter describes two tests of wills: between Rachel and Leah, and between Laban and Jacob. In fact, this is an important chapter in the mounting tension and conflict of the Genesis story. We began with the conflict between Sarah and Hagar. Then came the conflict of Isaac's household, between Esau and Jacob. After the present chapter it will continue in the accounts of Jacob's family, eventually leading to Joseph's being sold by his brothers into slavery. Among the patriarchs there seems to have been precious little domestic tranquility. If one is looking for something along the lines of "The Secret to a Happy Family Life," Genesis is generally not much help.

At the end of chapter 29 the competition between Leah and Rachel was going strongly in favor of the former. She has four sons to Rachel's none as chapter 30 begins. Growing rather desperate (vv. 1–2), Rachel resorts to a tactic earlier employed by Sarah; this legal fiction is well attested in the extant literature of that time and period, specifically the Nuzi Tablets from excavations near the Tigris River.

Rachel's plan, which effectively gives Jacob a third wife, works to her advantage (vv. 3–8). Two can play that game, thinks Leah, who promptly follows the same tack (vv. 9–12). Now Jacob has four wives and eight sons. Very quickly, however, the two sisters go beyond the niceties of the law. Leah resorts to a fertility drug (vv. 13–21) and bears two more sons and a daughter. At last Rachel has a son (vv. 22–24), whose story will dominate the final chapters of Genesis.

The relationship between Laban and Jacob has been something of a domestic business arrangement all along. For all legal and practical purposes, Jacob has become Laban's son and heir. Meanwhile, however, everything still belongs to Laban. When Jacob asks to have a little something for himself (vv. 25–34), he appears to be requesting a mere pittance, because in the Middle East the sheep are normally white and the goats normally black. Speckled and spotted animals are the exception. Laban, however, takes steps to eliminate even that pittance (vv. 35–36).

Meanwhile, Jacob, having grown a great deal smarter, has plans of his own (vv. 37–43). In putting three days' distance between his own herds and those shepherded by Jacob, Laban intends to keep the speckled goats and the dark sheep away from him. This plan backfires, because it permits Jacob to have a three-days' jump on Laban when it comes time to leave.

⌒ Genesis 31 ⌒

When Jacob wanted to leave in the previous chapter, it was his own idea. As we commence the present chapter, however, the initiative comes from God (vv. 1–13).

Jacob summons his wives away from the tents and the ears of inquisitive servants who might report the discussion back to Laban. His argument is twofold, both earthly and heavenly. In purely earthly terms, he is fed up with working for Laban. As regards the heavenly, Jacob has heard from the God who had revealed Himself earlier, the "God of Bethel," *El-Bethel*. That God had earlier promised to bring him back home (28:15), and now He is fulfilling that promise (vv. 3, 13).

It turns out that Laban's daughters are none too happy with their father's treatment either. In his injustice to Jacob, Laban has also been unjust to his own flesh. He has treated them, not as daughters, but as outsiders. He not only *sold* them to Jacob; he has already used up the money he got for them! Leah and Rachel do not agree about much, but they do agree that it is time to start thinking of the welfare of their own children (vv. 14–18). They flee (vv. 19–21).

When Laban overtakes them (vv. 22–32), his complaints seem natural enough: "I did not get to say goodbye. I did not get to kiss my grandchildren. I did not get a chance to throw a going-away party. How could you treat me like this after all these years?"

Somebody in Jacob's party (and the reader already knows who) has, in addition, pilfered one of Laban's household gods. This incident does say something about the introduction of idolatry into the family, a problem that will prove to be chronic in biblical history. Holy Scripture provides numerous instances of idolatry introduced into Israel by the wives of Israel's kings (cf. 3 Kingdoms 15:13, for instance).

To cover her tracks, Rachel resorts to a ruse (vv. 33–37), concerning which two points should be made. First, the reader is expected to be amused that a god is being sat upon. Second, there seems to be no end of deception in this family!

Feeling vindicated by Laban's failure to find the absconded god, Jacob then upbraids his father-in-law, laying it on pretty thick (vv. 43–54). It is a masterpiece of self-justification, in which the speaker is manifestly enjoying himself. Indeed, the author intends for the reader to enjoy it too.

By ascribing all his success to God, Jacob also intends to make Laban pause for thought; does Laban really want to be tough on someone whom God favors? Laban, evidently chagrined at not finding the stolen god, is at some disadvantage; he is unable to answer Jacob. The two men make a covenant and call it a day (vv. 41–54). Laban and Jacob both head for home.

Excursus:
Jacob & Odysseus
I propose here to compare the biblical Jacob to the Greek hero Odysseus, who represents in classical

Greek literature a place analogous to that of Jacob in the Hebrew Bible.

We may begin by recalling that the Greeks were not agreed what to make of Odysseus. A "very versatile man" (*aner polytropos*), as Homer called him, expert in ruse and a master of disguise, this son and heir of Laertes was certainly among the most interesting and entertaining characters in classical memory. Both sagacious in counsel and brave in combat, moreover, his role in the routing of Troy placed Odysseus with the heroes honored in the annals of valor.

Some Greeks, nonetheless, did not feel entirely comfortable with this cunning warrior, "ever resourceful" (*polymetis*), never at a loss for the ingenious plan or the artful word. Even while admiring his various stratagems—his clever escape from the Cyclops's cave, for instance—they wondered if all that talented guile was entirely a good thing. Was there not something rather sneaky, duplicitous, and a tad too fast about it all? Indeed, might there not be some deeper significance in the fact (proved in the footrace at the funeral games of Patroclus) that Odysseus was simply much faster than everyone else?

Even conceding that Odysseus would never have arrived safely back home in Ithaca except for that wild, wily aspect of his character, was a man of so much deception to be held up for the emulation of the young? Were the ways of guile to be regarded as models in education? Would the imitation of shrewd Odysseus lead to a more virtuous citizenry and the enhancement of public trust? Doubting it, Pindar and Sophocles expressed their reservations about Odysseus. Plato, in fact, raised those same questions in the shorter dialogue between Socrates and Hippias, which contrasted the cunning of Odysseus with the candor of honest Achilles. In short, the example of Odysseus was a bit of a problem.

Now, with no possible rival, I think, the Odysseus in the Bible is Jacob. Truth to tell, the several parallels between the two are very striking, if not always edifying. For starts, both characters were utter con men, unscrupulous deceivers, fluent, even eloquent, in falsehood. The one tricked blind Polyphemus by hiding under a sheep, while the other deceived his blind father by hiding under a goatskin. Both moreover were blessed by blind men, the one by blind Teiresias, the other by blind Isaac. Each man struck a deal to win his wife, the one with Tyndareus, the other with Laban. The one profited from the herds of Helios, the other from the flocks of his father-in-law.

Both Odysseus and Jacob, furthermore, were accomplished, wide-ranging travelers. Whereas Odysseus returned home in disguise, Jacob left home because of a disguise. In the course of those journeys, the reader is struck by the attention given to events that happened while the two travelers slept, whether near Aeolia and at the Bay of Porcys, or at Bethel and the ford at Peniel. Both travelers, likewise, left aging fathers, but even after many years each returned to find his father still alive. Indeed, the paternal home was the goal of each man's journey.

Jacob's flamboyant career began even in his mother's womb, where he and his twin brother wrestled to see who would be born first. Esau won the match, but Jacob emerged still clinging to his sibling's heel, determined never to lose again. He seldom did. Many years later he would walk with a limp from an injury sustained in another wrestling match, that time with an angel. Jacob won that contest too.

But God sees all things, including the future, and He knew how Jacob would turn out in the end. God foresaw the finishing days of an old man finally purified by much pain. God foreknew the aging heart chastened by grief for a lost son and disappointment in the other sons. God saw, already, the latter exile of Jacob in the land of Egypt, much humbled now, long bereft of the woman he really loved, and waiting to die on alien soil. God could hear already the much wiser ancient who told Pharaoh, "The days of the years of my sojourn are one hundred and thirty years; few and evil have they been; but they have not attained to the days and years of my father's sojourn in life" (47:9).

ᴄ: GENESIS 32 :~

After taking leave of Laban, Jacob must think about how to approach Esau, for Esau represents the tricky aspect of Jacob's homecoming (vv. 4–7). Esau, meanwhile, has moved south to the land of Edom, a dry and inhospitable land that lucidly explains the words of God, "Esau I have hated, and I have appointed his borders for destruction and made his heritage as dwellings of the wilderness" (Malachi 1:3).

If Jacob is feeling threatened by Laban, he now feels even worse from the information that his older twin is coming to meet him with four hundred armed men. That last part is hardly the sort of detail calculated to allay anxiety. Indeed, a certain sense of anxiety may be exactly what Esau wants to inspire in Jacob. If so, the maneuver is successful.

Jacob does two things (vv. 8–13). First, he prepares for the worst, taking certain practical steps with a view to at least a partial survival of his family. Second, he takes to prayer, certainly the most humble prayer he has made so far.

Ultimately, after all, this is a story of Jacob's relationship to God. Up to this point, God is still Isaac's God, the "God of my fathers" (v. 9). Jacob has not yet done what he promised at Bethel—take God as his own (28:21). God had also made certain promises to Jacob at Bethel, and Jacob now invokes those promises.

He continues his preparations for meeting the brother he has not seen in twenty years (vv. 14–23). He sends delegations with gifts, which are intended to impress Esau. Jacob, after all, knows that Esau has four hundred men, but Esau does not know how many Jacob may have. Jacob's gifts, including five hundred and eighty animals, verge on the flamboyant.

Jacob approaches the ford of Jabbok, at a place called Peniel, or "face of God" (v. 30). The Hebrew text of verses 17–31 uses the word "face" (*paneh*) no fewer than six times. Jacob knows that Esau will soon be "in his face." He must "face" Esau, which is why he is going directly toward him. Up to this point, Jacob has been a man of flight, flight from Canaan, flight from Haran, flight from Esau, flight from Laban. This all must change. Jacob cannot face his future until he has faced his past.

Even before he can face Esau, however, Jacob must face Someone Else (vv. 23–33). This encounter with God, which apparently Jacob has not anticipated, is far more significant than his encounter with Esau. A millennium later the prophet Hosea would meditate on this scene. This wrestling match is Jacob's decisive encounter with God. Everything changes. First, his name is changed to Israel (v. 29), as Abram's was changed to Abraham in a parallel encounter with God (17:3–5, 15). Second, God is no longer simply "the God of my fathers." He is now "the God of Israel" (v. 20). Third, Jacob will limp from this experience for the rest of his life (vv. 26, 32–33). No one wrestles with the living God and afterwards looks normal and well-adjusted. There is a further irony here. Jacob began life by tripping his brother as the latter exited the womb. Now Jacob himself will be permanently tripped up by a limp.

Jacob has remained on the near side of the river all night long, not fording the Jabbok with the rest of his family. When he rises in the morning, he must limp across alone. Esau and his four hundred men are just coming into view.

⁓: GENESIS 33 :⁓

One is struck by Jacob's great deference to his older brother, whom he had severely wronged a couple of decades earlier (vv. 1–4). As it turned out, however, it was not necessary for Jacob to appease Esau. Even without his primogeniture inheritance and the blessing of the firstborn, Esau had done very well for himself and appeared not to hold a grudge against his brother. Evidently the blessing that Isaac pronounced over Esau was very potent (27:39).

Esau meets the rest of the family (vv. 4–7), and all manner of politeness is exchanged (vv. 8–11). Stress is laid on the great wealth of each of the brothers, in terms that may remind the reader of Solomon later on (1 Kings 10:14–25).

Esau is concerned for Jacob's safety as he travels with considerable wealth but with no adequate military escort. Jacob moves on, however, and settles down for some time at Succoth (vv. 12–17). He eventually goes to Shechem (the modern Nablus, a corruption of the Greek *neapolis* or "new city"). There he builds a shrine (vv. 18–20).

Comparing the present account with Jacob's earlier prayer at Bethel in chapter 28, we observe in him a new level of spiritual maturity. Whereas in that earlier scene the Lord had identified Himself as "the Lord God of Abraham your father and the God of Isaac" (28:13), in the present text the shrine is dedicated to *El Elohe Israel*, "God, the God of Israel." The God of Jacob's fathers has now truly become his own God. This designation reflects Jacob's experience at Peniel, where he wrestled with the Almighty and received a new name. The Bible's next story will find Jacob still at Shechem.

So far we have found the patriarchs associated with most of the great cultic centers of the Holy Land, such as Hebron, Beersheba, Bethel, and Shechem.

∾ GENESIS 34 ∾

The other inhabitants of Shechem are called Hivites in the Hebrew text, Hurrians or Horites in the Greek text. Non-Semites, they did not practice circumcision, and their introduction to the practice will be something less than felicitous.

Jacob's daughter went gadding about (vv. 1–4) and came to the attention of a local young man who was evidently accustomed to getting what he wanted. His name was Shechem too. In spite of the

New American Bible's indication of violence ("he lay with her by force"), the Hebrew *wai'anneha* is perhaps better translated as "he humbled her" or "he seduced her." Subsequent events suggest that this was not an act of violence. As it turns out, in fact, Dinah is already living at the young man's home.

We noted that this young Shechem was accustomed to getting what he wanted. Now he is about to be introduced to Dinah's big brothers, who have some ideas of their own and also know what they want. This will be Israel's first recorded armed conflict. As in the case of the Greeks assembled before the walls of Troy, they will be fighting over a stolen woman.

Down through the centuries this biblical story has been told chiefly for its moral message. For instance, in the twelfth century St. Bernard of Clairvaux used Dinah as an example of a gadabout, exemplifying the vice of curiosity, which Bernard called "the first step" on the inversed ladder of pride.

Jacob and Hamor, the fathers of the two young people, are remarkably patient, but not Dinah's brothers (vv. 5–7). As we shall see in the cases of Reuben and Judah in the next few chapters, Jacob's sons are not all models of chastity, but they were genuinely concerned for their sister's well-being and their family's honor. To describe what has happened to Dinah, they employ the word *nebelah* or "folly," which term rather often indicates a sexual offense. For instance, this word appears four times in Judges 19—20, where it refers to a woman's being raped to death. It also refers to Amnon's rape of Tamar in 2 Kingdoms 13:12, to adultery in Jeremiah 29:23, and to the infidelity of an engaged girl in Deuteronomy 22:21. The word is perhaps better translated as "outrage."

A meeting takes place, as though by accident (vv. 8–12). Hamor and Shechem offer a deal. After all, Dinah is living at Shechem's house. Why not simply legitimize the situation? Any solution but marriage would make things worse. Besides, the Shechemites reason, if they were all going to be neighbors anyway, why not a general miscegenation of the two peoples?

Here we touch upon an important point of theology, because the very concept of intermarriage might mean that the line of Abraham, Isaac, and Jacob would cease to be distinct; the very notion of a chosen people might be lost. Intermarriage with these Shechemites would have led to quite another result than that envisioned in the Bible (cf. 2 Corinthians 6:14–18).

Jacob's sons make a reasonable proposal, but not sincerely (vv. 13–17). They speak "with guile," *bemirmah*. This is the identical expression we saw in 27:35 to describe what Jacob had done: "Your brother came *bemirmah* and has taken away your blessing." Guile seems to run in this family.

Shechem's family, anyway, agree to submit to circumcision (vv. 18–24). Do they realize that they will thereby be accepting the covenant in chapter 17? Probably not, but the question is moot anyway. Circumcision is simply part of a deceitful plan in this instance.

The sin of Simeon and Levi (vv. 25–29), in addition to its cruelty, has about it a touch of deep irreverence. God gave Abraham's sons the rite of circumcision as the sign of a special covenant. That is to say, circumcision was God's chosen sign for blessing. By their actions in this chapter, Simeon and Levi distort that sign, turning it into an occasion of violence against their enemies. They take something sacred and transform it into the instrument of their own vengeance. Their action in this case points to the danger of using the blessings of God *against* our fellow man.

ᴄ: GENESIS 35 :~

Jacob revisits Bethel (vv. 1–7), a story that continues the tough "reform" mentality of the previous chapter. Bethel represents, after all, Jacob's acceptance of personal monotheism: "There is only one God, and He is my God."

The washing and changing of clothing is symbolic of Jacob's sense of the holiness of the place (Exodus 19:10), and those earrings are crescents dedicated to the Semitic moon divinity.

Verse 8 is a sort of parenthesis; that is, the author, when he comes to speak of Bethel, suddenly remembers that the nurse of Jacob's mother was buried there. Otherwise, this verse seems to have no connection at all to the narrative at this stage.

The promises of the covenant are renewed for Jacob (vv. 9–10). The scene is reminiscent of similar covenant scenes with Abraham (15:5, 7) and Isaac (26:2–4).

Bethel had been the scene of an earlier "stage" in Jacob's religious growth. His return there (vv. 13–15) indicates that that earlier stage must now be incorporated into the larger picture. Jacob goes back to rethink and to rededicate that earlier event. In a sense, he is no longer the same man who first went to Bethel. Yet, that earlier event was an essential component of what Jacob has now become.

Finally we come to the birth of Benjamin and the death of Rachel (vv. 16–20), Jacob's favorite wife. Benjamin is the only one of Jacob's sons to be born in the Holy Land. His mother's choice for the boy's name, Benomi, meant either "son of my strength" or, more likely, "son of my affliction." The name Benjamin means "right-hand son." This could mean something close to our own metaphor of "my right-hand man," or it could simply mean "southerner" (for an "oriented" or east-facing person). If this latter signification is what is intended, it may mean that Benjamin was born the furthest south of all the sons of Jacob. Whatever the specific meaning, the reader should not forget that we are reading here the partial genealogy of the apostle Paul (cf. Romans 11:1; Philippians 3:3–4).

Another domestic scandal ensues (vv. 21–22), this time respecting Reuben. The latter will later come in for a rather unfavorable mention because of this incident (49:3–4), and in fact the tribe of Reuben will never amount to much in Israel's history. In due course it will be absorbed by the Gadites and the tribe of Manasseh, and poor Reuben will be left with only a sandwich named after him.

In the patriarchal list that follows (vv. 27–29), the author of Genesis is telling us that the foundation has now been laid for the rest of the biblical story. The patriarchal roots are now in place. We may compare this "list of the Twelve" with the four Gospels and the Acts of the Apostles, which early provide lists of the Twelve Apostles. In all these cases, as here in Genesis, we are dealing with a patriarchal institution.

Finally, we come to the death of Isaac (vv. 27–29). Isaac thought he was dying back in 27:4, but here he is, eight chapters later, still alive, up to the end of chapter 35. Isaac was already 60 years old when the twins were born (25:26) and a hundred years old when Esau first married (26:34), and another eighty years have passed since *then* (v. 28).

ᙍ GENESIS 36 ᙍ

Before closing the door on Esau, who was rejected from a direct and active role in salvation history (Malachi 1:2–3; Romans 9:13), the Bible provides its readers with a list of the tribes derived from the seed of Jacob's older brother, the peoples of Edom. This list forms a sort of literary break between the Jacob and Joseph cycles.

Were it not for the Bible, and this list in particular, the Edomites would have disappeared from recorded history just as surely as their patriarch disappeared from salvation history. The substance of this list was later incorporated into the work of the Chronicler (1 Chronicles 1:35–53).

This compilation appears to be made up of six separate lists: (1) the immediate sons of Esau and his settling at Seir (vv. 1–8); (2) Esau's grandsons (vv. 9–14); (3) the early chieftains of Edom (vv. 15–19); (4) the first inhabitants of Seir (vv. 20–30); (5) the kings of Edom (vv. 31–39); (6) the governors of Edom after their monarchy (vv. 40–43). The reader observes that these lists correspond to the developing stages of Edom's political history. That is to say, the biblical historians kept a steady eye on the Edomites over a fairly long history. (Much of this material obviously comes from periods long after Moses.)

In the first list (vv. 1–8) it is easy to discern small discrepancies with the narratives about Esau (26:34; 28:9). These are probably to be explained by discrepancies within the extrabiblical sources used in their compilation. Nor do all the biblical sources themselves agree on the names of Esau's wives. For example, in the Samaritan text Mahaleth is substituted for Basemath in vv. 3, 4, 10, 13, and 17. There is no substantial reason to suppose that Esau had more than three wives.

Some names in the second list (vv. 9–14) appear elsewhere in Holy Scripture. Reuel (v. 13), for instance, was the father-in-law of Moses (Exodus 2:18; Numbers 10:29), and Eliphaz (v. 12) may be one of the comforters of Job.

The tribal leaders in the third list (vv. 15–19) perhaps correspond to the period of the biblical "judges," on the reasonable hypothesis that Edom's political history rather closely matched that of Israel.

The fourth list (vv. 20–30), on the other hand, contains

information about the pre-Edomite inhabitants of Seir, the Horites. They are listed here only to fill out the genealogical picture of the region. Thus, the mention of Uz (v. 28) likely refers to the founder of the city called by that name, the hometown of Job.

The fifth list (vv. 31–39), which chronologically follows the third, contains the names of Edom's kings and presumably corresponds, in rough fashion, to Israel's monarchical period (1000–587 BC). The short sixth list of Edom's governors (vv. 40–43) apparently comes from the Persian period when the Edomites, like Israel, no longer had kings.

Notwithstanding the obvious sympathy toward Edomites demonstrated in the preservation of these lists, Israel's relationships with this people were anything but harmonious. Although the prophet Obadiah is perhaps our clearest example of an entirely negative sentiment toward Edom, he was scarcely alone in this respect. There is evidence that more than one Israelite found his style cramped by Deuteronomy's injunction not to despise the Edomite (Deuteronomy 23:7). Those descendants of Esau, after all, had obstructed the chosen people's way to the Promised Land in the days of Moses (Numbers 20:21), and according to the prophet Amos in the eighth century the Edomites, having "cast off all pity" (Amos 1:11, NKJV), were involved in international slave trade (1:6, 9).

Edom's most memorable offenses, however, occurred when the Babylonians destroyed Jerusalem in 587 BC. At that time they rejoiced at the city's downfall (Lamentations 4:21), exploiting its misfortune in a vengeful way (Ezekiel 25:12). Most serious of all was the vile complicity of the Edomites in the demolition of Solomon's temple, an outrage for which they are explicitly blamed in 1 Ezra 4:45. This final offense likewise inspired a line of Psalm 136(137), a lament composed in captivity "by the rivers of Babylon" (v. 1) where the exiles sat and wept, remembering Zion. Reflecting on the holy city's recent, ruthless destruction, the psalmist bitterly recalled Edom's share in the matter: "O Lord, remember the sons of Edom / On that day in Jerusalem, / When they were saying, 'Empty it out, / Empty it out, / Even to its foundation!'" (v. 7).

Obadiah's postexilic prophecy testifies that his own rancor toward the Edomites was prompted by the identical recollection. He particularly blames them for rejoicing at Jerusalem's downfall, despoiling the city, blocking the path of escape against those who fled, and handing the refugees over to their captors (Obadiah 12–14). He can scarcely forget that the descendants of Esau were, in fact, blood relatives of the Israelites. Like Amos, who had earlier accused Edom of pursuing "his brother with a sword" (Amos 1:11), Obadiah speaks of "slaughter and ungodliness against your brother Jacob" (Obadiah 10).

The prophetic doom pronounced by the Bible against the Edomites was vindicated in their displacement by the Nabateans in the fourth century BC. Forced to migrate to southern Palestine, they were eventually subjugated by John Hyrcanus (134–104 BC). From that point on, they were simply assimilated into Judaism. One of them, named Herod, even became a king of the Jews, but he always sensed that someday a real descendant of David might appear on the scene and challenge his claim to the throne. It made him very nervous and unreasonable.

PART SIX
THE JOSEPH CYCLE

∾ GENESIS 37 ∾

Any reader of Genesis with even a little feel for structure and style will recognize that he has arrived at something new when he starts through the long Joseph narrative. Although all of the stories in Genesis are tied together by unifying historico-theological themes and a panoramic epic construction, there are two very clear points of style in which this long story of Joseph stands out unique with respect to the narratives that precede it.

The first stylistic point has to do with structure. The various accounts of Abraham, Isaac, and Jacob have what we may call a more episodic quality. Even though they are integrally tied together by theological motifs and theme-threads indispensable to their full meaning, often they can also be read as individual stories, each with a satisfying dramatic anatomy of its own. For example, while the more ample significance of Abraham's trial in chapter 22 doubtless requires its integration into the larger motif of the Promised Son and Heir, that chapter is so constructed that it may also be read as a single story with its own inherent drama. That is to say, it is an episode. Part of its literary quality consists in its being intelligible and interesting within itself and on its own merits.

Similar assessments are likewise true for numerous other patriarchal stories, including the rivalry between Sarah and Hagar, the courting of Rebekah, Jacob's theft of Esau's blessing, and so forth. While parts of a larger whole, each of these narratives nonetheless forms a good, satisfactory dramatic tale by itself.

There is nothing similar in the Joseph narrative. Hardly any scene of the Joseph narrative could stand alone and still make sense. It is one and only one story. No one of the parts is of interest without the rest.

The Joseph epic forms one long dramatic unity, characterized by the careful planning of particulars, sustained irony, a very tight integration of component scenes within a tension mounting to a dramatic denouement, followed by a more quiet sequence that calmly closes Genesis and systematically prepares for the Book of Exodus.

The second stylistic point that distinguishes the Joseph story from the earlier Genesis stories is the quality of its interest in the dominant character. The sensitive reader of Genesis will note right away that Joseph appears to have no failings nor faults, in sharp contrast to the earlier patriarchal figures. Both Abraham and Isaac, for example, acting from fear of possible rivals, go to some lengths to suggest that they are *not* married to their wives (12:11–19; 20:2–13; 26:7–11), a precaution that seems, at the very least, to fall somewhat short of the ideals of chivalry. Similarly, Jacob's intentional deception of his father in chapter 27 is scarcely edifying, while the cunning brutality of Simeon and Levi in chapter 34 is lamented by Jacob himself. The Bible is obviously making no attempt to glorify those men; it simply portrays them as mixtures of good and evil, very much as we should expect from any accurate biography.

There is a perceptible change of attitude, however, when we come to Joseph. Genesis offers, I think, no parallel example of such a sustained interest in describing the moral shape of a specific character. Joseph is pictured as a flawless or nearly flawless man. He seems almost a type of perfection, a veritable saint right from the start. The Fathers of the Church could thus hold Joseph up as an example of humility,[1] chastity,[2] prudent foresight,[3] and inner discipline of thought. He was "that very man of God, full of the spirit of discretion," wrote Gregory Dialogos.[4]

---

1   Ambrose, *Epistolae* 2.19–22; 37.9–10; Augustine, *De Civitate Dei* 18.4; Gregory Dialogos, *Moralium,* Praef. 6.13

2   Basil, *Epistolae* 2.3; 46.4; Gregory the Theologian, *Orationes Theologicae* 24.13; Zeno of Verona, *Tractactus* 1.4; Ambrose, *In Psalmum* CXVIII 15.11; *In Lucam* 3.47; *De Officiis* 1.17.66; 2.5.19 (108C); *Exhortatio Virginitatis* 13.88; *Epistolae* 48.12; John Chrysostom, *In Primam ad Thessalonicenses* 4.5; *Homiliae in Genesim* 62.4; Augustine, *Sermones* 318.2

3   Ambrose, *De Officiis* 2.16; Gregory Dialogos, *Epistolae* 35

4   *In Ezechielem* 2.9.19

Likewise, Joseph's ability to discern the future makes him the Bible's earliest clear example of a prophet.[5] In his patient suffering, moreover, his endurance of betrayal, his confidence in God's guidance and his forgiveness of those who wronged him, Joseph seemed to the Church Fathers to embody the highest ideals of the Gospel itself.[6]

This "hagiographical" approach is rare in scriptural narrative, the other few examples that come readily to mind being only Jonathan, Nehemiah, Daniel, Tobit, and perhaps Stephen. Most of the biblical personalities, after all, are composites of good and bad, mixtures of strength and weakness, with which most of us more easily identify our own experience: Abraham, Jacob, David, Jeremiah, Jonah, Peter and the other apostles, and so forth. It is understandable we find ourselves more in sympathy with these latter figures, and their use throughout the history of Christian ascetical literature amply justifies our doing so.

Nonetheless, it seems important to observe that the more idealized picture of the "saint" also has biblical roots. For example, the "cloud of witnesses" in Hebrews 11 is sufficiently cloudy to leave out all mention of the weaknesses and failings of its numerous characters, instead concentrating entirely on their faith. Such a hagiographical disposition is already at work in the Genesis narrative of Joseph.

Excursus:
Potiphar's Wife

Among the stories in Genesis more easily remembered—even if only for being a bit racy—is the one about Joseph's temptation by Potiphar's wife

---

5 Basil, *In Isaiam, Proem.* 4; Ambrose, *De Joseph Patriarcha* 3.9; Augustine, *De Genesi ad Litteram* 12.9.20; Prosper of Aquitaine, *Expositio Psalmorum* 104; Procopius of Gaza, *In Isaiam, Proem.*

6 Clement of Rome 4; Cyprian, *De Bono Patientiae* 10; *De Zelo et Livore* 5; Zeno of Verona, *Tractactus* 1.6; Cyril of Jerusalem, *Catechesis* 8.4; Ambrose, *In Psalmum* CXVIII 11.30; *De Officiis* 1.24.112; 2.11.59; 2.15.74; John Chrysostom, *In Secundam ad Thessalonicenses* 2.1; *Homiliae in Genesim* 63.2; Jerome, *In Ephesios* 3.5

(37:7–20). When the young man told her, "Oh no, ma'am, this is a really bad idea," the lady took the rejection personally, as they say, and went on to accuse Joseph of trying to seduce *her*. Joseph then was thrown in jail, until "The king, the ruler of the people, sent and released him, / And he acquitted him" (Psalm 104[105]:20).

The tale of Joseph and Potiphar's wife was not antiquity's sole narrative of a young man falsely accused by a married woman after resisting her adulterous enticements. An Egyptian manuscript, for example, closely dated to about 1225 BC (Papyrus D'Orbiney, British Museum 10183), records a strikingly similar story of two brothers and the wife of the older brother.

In this account, the younger brother, Bata, lived in the home of the older, Anubis, "as a sort of dependent," who did all the work on the farm. As Bata grew to full manhood, the wife of Anubis began to cast on this younger brother an ever more lustful eye. Like Joseph, Bata was physically attractive. Indeed, the text says, "There was no one like him in the entire land. Why, the strength of a god was in him." The wife of Anubis endeavored to seduce Bata, but he steadfastly resisted her allurements. Outraged at being thus scorned, she accused him of attempted rape. Anubis, of course, believed her.

The several similarities between this tale and the Joseph story are all the more striking inasmuch as both accounts come from the same time (late second millennium BC) and place (Egypt).

The theme was hardly limited to Egypt, however. Homer (*Iliad* 6.150–168) told an almost identical story of "peerless Bellerophon," to whom "the gods granted beauty and manly appeal. The wife of Proteus, lovely Anteia, longed with mad passion to lie in secret love" with Bellerophon. Her efforts, however, were wasted on "wise Bellerophon, who discerned what was proper." Like Mrs. Potiphar, Anteia then accused the young man of attempting to seduce her, and Proteus, like Potiphar, believed his wife.

This pattern is found repeatedly in classical literature. Thus Apollodorus tells the tale of young Peleus, who was indicted by Cretheis, the wife of Acastus, when he declined her advances. Pausanias similarly tells of the wife of Crethesus, Biadice, who lusted after handsome Phrixus and, when he rebuffed her, mendaciously accused him. Both Apollodorus and Pausanias write of Tenes, who was tempted by Philonome, the wife of Cycnus. When the young man withstood her charms, Philonome retaliated by charging him with attempted rape. Ovid and others tell the story of Hippolytus, against whom Phaedra, the wife of Theseus, brought the same accusation after her unsuccessful attempt at seduction.

Within the common pattern of all these stories, the names themselves are nearly interchangeable. There is invariably an innocent young, unmarried man—call him Joseph, Bata, Peleus, or whatever—who unwittingly catches the roaming eye of an older, more experienced, married woman. She, endeavoring to seduce the young fellow, is scorned, and in revenge she falsely accuses *him* of being the seducer.

Although most of these stories are preserved in mythology where they do not serve an explicitly moral purpose, they can all certainly be read for that purpose, and the moral lesson thus derived is identical in each. Namely, a young man receives the very sound counsel that he must "keep yourself from a married woman / And from the slanderous tongue of a strange woman" (Proverbs 6:29). This is a very old theme in Wisdom literature. An ancient Akkadian text (*A Pessimistic Dialogue Between Master and Servant*) refers to such a woman as "a sharp iron dagger that cuts a man's neck." In cases like this, mere exhortations to chastity are not enough. What is required is swift and decisive flight.

In the story of Joseph the theme of Wisdom is explicit and pronounced (41:39; Psalms 104 [105]:22), and here Potiphar's wife serves as the very incarnation of Dame Folly, that quintessential adventuress trying to seduce the inexperienced young man (Proverbs 5:3–6, 20; 6:29–40; 7:5–6). As Joseph learned to his considerable hurt, it was in reference to Potiphar's wife and residence that the wise man was warned, "Make your way distant from her / And do not come near the doors of her house" (Proverbs 5:8).

❧ GENESIS 38 ❧

Although this last section of Genesis centers on Joseph, the text does not lose sight of the bigger picture, the bigger picture here understood as the entire biblical message. In that bigger picture, Judah plays a more important role than Joseph. Ultimately the descendants of Joseph, the tribes of Ephraim and Manasseh, pertain to the ten lost tribes, whereas the tribe of Judah will provide the royal house of David and the Messiah (49:8–10; Matthew 2:6; Revelation 5:5). It is ultimately Judah who will give the "Jews" their name.

Between chapters 37 and 45, some twenty years elapse, and a significant number of those years are required by the events in chapter 38. Hence, this chapter allows the reader to put Joseph out of his mind for a while. It is something of an interlude, permitting Joseph to become settled in Egypt. It is a "here and there" style of narrative, inserted to fill in a gap and convey the impression of the passage of time until the thread of the larger narrative is taken up again. (Other biblical examples of this technique must include the narrative between Mark 6:7 and 30, contrasted with that of Luke 9:2 and 10).

The interest of this chapter, however, is less in Judah as a person than in Judah as the father of his tribe. In the larger picture this is a story about Judah's descendants. Since it is the story of his lineage, it must start by getting him married (vv. 1–5). This family too has its problems (vv. 6–11). Once again there is a deception by means of disguise, an unfortunate characteristic which, as we have seen, tends to run in the family (vv. 12–19).

We note that the Bible is not hard on Tamar here; she is simply trying to get what she has coming to her—namely, children. Judah, thinking he has managed to avoid Tamar all those years, now discovers an easy way to get rid of her for good (vv. 24–26), but the young lady turns the tables on him. There is nothing Judah can do but acknowledge his paternity and get on with life.

This story is, in addition, one of the Bible's great accounts of an underdog getting back at an oppressor. In this respect, Tamar's story runs parallel with those of Esther and Judith. The irony of it continues into the New Testament, where Tamar enters the genealogy of the Savior (Matthew 1:5).

ᕙ GENESIS 39 ᕗ

The story of Joseph is staged in various ways. For example, Joseph's different changes of fortune are symbolized in his clothing. His famous and elaborate tunic, which focuses the hatred of his brothers in 37:3f, is dipped in blood in 37:23–32, thus symbolizing Joseph's alienation from his family. Then, in vv. 12–18 of the present chapter, his ill-fated encounter with Potiphar's wife is imaged in the loss of the cloak used as evidence to imprison him. His eventual release from prison will again involve a change of clothing in 41:14, and finally a whole new wardrobe symbolizes his new state in 41:42.

Another element of staging and cohesion in the story is introduced by Joseph's two dreams in 37:5–10, in each of which his brothers bow down before him. This double prostration is prophetic, inasmuch as the brothers bow before him on each of their trips to Egypt (42:6; 43:26; 44:14; 50:18), and Joseph specifically remembers the dreams on the first of these instances (42:9).

The Joseph narrative is one of the Bible's first examples of a story happening in two places at once. The introduction of the Judah episode in chapter 38, right after Joseph's departure for Egypt, serves to suggest a lengthy passage of time, but it also establishes what will become a mounting "geographical" tension between dual centers of activity, Canaan and Egypt. The journeys of the brothers to Egypt and their returns to Canaan will eventually provide the setting for the two conflicting aspirations of Joseph and Jacob, the former resolved to bring Benjamin to Egypt, and the latter determined to keep him in Canaan.

How does Joseph survive all those years in Egypt? Surely by his reliance on the providence of God. This was the secret of Joseph's inner life. It explains both his patience in tribulation and his ready forgiveness of enemies. Even as a slave, even in prison, Joseph was an inwardly free man, said St. Cyril of Alexandria (*In Joannem* 5.8.36), and Procopius of Gaza (*In Genesim* 50) wrote that Joseph was perpetually and prayerfully mindful of the presence of God.

∽ GENESIS 40 ∾

The climax of the Joseph story will be his revelation of himself to his brothers. Everything in the story is arranged to set up that event. Thus, Joseph must go to jail. If he does not go to jail, he will not meet the king's cupbearer. If he does not meet the king's cupbearer, he will not come to the attention of Pharaoh. If he is not brought to the attention of Pharaoh, he will not encounter his brothers. And so on. The narrative is thus very carefully pieced together.

Meanwhile, Joseph is in jail. Indeed, he is pretty much running the place after a while (39:23), when two other prisoners are brought in (vv. 1–4). Already introduced to the reader as a man of dreams in chapter 37, Joseph now appears as an interpreter of dreams (vv. 4–8).

A royal cupbearer was a great deal more than a table servant. He was, rather, a high official of the court, normally ranking right after the royal family itself. Such men were obliged to be very careful, for they served autocratic masters and were perpetually in danger of offending them (cf. Nehemiah 1:11—2:6). Somehow or other, this cupbearer had managed to offend Pharaoh. Thrown in jail, he had done a lot of brooding, and this brooding led to a dream about his fate (vv. 9–11). Joseph's interpretation of the dream, however, is rather encouraging (vv. 12–13). The Hebrew in this passage says that the cupbearer's head will be "lifted up." In this instance, to "lift up the head" means to exalt, to restore to honor. Even as Joseph gives the cupbearer his interpretation of the dream, he senses that this gentleman may someday provide his own way out of prison (vv. 14–15).

Encouraged by Joseph's interpretation of the cupbearer's dream, the royal baker decides to tell his own dream (vv. 16–17). The images in each dream are related to the professions of the dreamers, pressed grapes and cup for the first man, baskets of bakery goods for the second. In each case, the number "three" is important. This second dream, nonetheless, introduces a disturbing note: Birds come and peck at the baked goods. This is an alien element, a common symbol of frustration in dreams.

Joseph sees right away that this is not a good sign (vv. 18–19). In the Hebrew text, there is a rather grim play on words here, a feature not conveyed in the Septuagint translation. "Lifting up the head" no longer implies restoration and exaltation as it did in the cupbearer's dream. The baker's head will be "lifted up," rather, in the sense that he will be decapitated. Understandably, we observe that the baker neglects to thank Joseph for this interpretation of his dream!

The important point is that Joseph's interpretations of the two dreams are prophetic (vv. 20–23). The next chapter will tell us, however, that the cupbearer will not remember Joseph for another two years.

❧ GENESIS 41 ☙

We now come to the third discussion of dreams in the Joseph story. Pharaoh has a dream. Indeed, it becomes something of a nightmare, causing Pharaoh to wake up, which is perhaps why he can recall the dream so vividly (vv. 1–4). Going back to sleep, he has another dream (vv. 5–7).

It is interesting that Herodotus (2.136) provides us with a story that parallels the present instance. It concerns the dream of an Ethiopian pharaoh named Shabaka, of the twenty-fifth dynasty (725–667 BC). Egyptian literature itself is full of such dreams. In antiquity dreams were regarded as among the ways that gods revealed practical truths to kings and other leaders. We find another instance of it in the case of Solomon (3 Kingdoms 3; 2 Chronicles 1).

Pharaoh's two dreams have left him very upset, and at last the cupbearer remembers Joseph (vv. 8–13). After all, kings could become *very* upset if no one could be found to interpret their dreams (cf. Daniel 2:1–6). Evidently the cupbearer sensed danger, since Pharaoh's dream had not yet an interpreter. The fear serves to jog his memory; he recalls how he himself had gotten out of jail two years earlier. At this point he apparently does not even recall Joseph's name (v. 12).

Joseph is summoned (vv. 14–16). We note that this is the third reference to a change in Joseph's clothing.

Joseph has no doubt that this dream comes from God. God speaks to man in dreams (compare Job 33:15–18; Numbers 12:6). Pharaoh, then, tells his dreams (vv. 17–24). We observe that these dreams are not predictions; they are a diagnosis and a warning. Thus, Joseph is able, not only to interpret the dreams, but to instruct Pharaoh what to do about them. His wisdom, in other words, is not just speculative, but practical (vv. 25–32).

Pharaoh's dreams have to do with the Nile River, the annual flooding of which is essential to Egyptian agriculture. The Nile's failure to flood over a seven-year period would be catastrophic indeed. In fact, there is a stone inscription found near the first cataract of the Nile, on the island of Siheil, which indicates that a seven-year drought was not unthinkable.

Joseph does not even pause (vv. 33–36). He immediately supplies the practical remedy for the problem, not even waiting for Pharaoh to question him. One has the impression that he has already worked out the details in his mind while he was giving Pharaoh the interpretation. There is no time to be lost (v. 32). The work will require centralized control. This is no work for a committee, and there is no time for a discussion. The only efficient course will require a strong, swift, executive hand (v. 33).

We have already seen Joseph as a take-charge kind of fellow, managing Potiphar's estate as soon as he arrived, put in direction of the jail as soon as he became a prisoner, and so forth. Pharaoh knows that he has before him the right man for the job (vv. 37–43), recognizing that this wisdom comes from the Holy Spirit (vv. 38–39).

Joseph again changes clothes (v. 42) and starts a new life (vv. 44–46), with new responsibilities (vv. 47–49). His plans are successful (vv. 53–57).

Joseph becomes the father of two Israelite tribes (vv. 50–52). According to Origen and other interpreters, he is now about thirty years old.

∾ GENESIS 42 ∾

The predicted famine also hits the land of Canaan, at which point the Joseph story is tied back to its earlier period (vv. 1–5). We learn right away that Jacob, having lost Joseph, has become excessively protective of his youngest son Benjamin. This detail is inserted early in the narrative sequence, because it will become an important component in the development of the story.

These next few chapters will be sustained by a tension between Egypt and Canaan, between Joseph and Jacob, with Joseph trying to get Benjamin down into Egypt, while Jacob endeavors to keep him in Canaan.

When the other brothers come into Egypt (vv. 6–7), Joseph starts his game, which begins by some fun at their expense. As we have seen, this kind of thing runs in the family. Abraham had deceived Pharaoh by claiming to be Sarah's brother. Isaac had deceived Abimelech by pretending to be Rebekah's brother. Jacob deceived Isaac by pretending to be Esau. Leah pretended to be Rachel, thereby deceiving Jacob. The Bible obviously revels in this sort of thing. Indeed, our eternal salvation itself will involve a massive act of deception, in which the Wisdom of God deceives Satan (1 Corinthians 2:6–8).

Without knowing who he is, the brothers prostrate themselves before Joseph (vv. 8–17), who recognizes in their act the fulfillment of dreams he had shared with them two decades earlier.

Even while deceiving his brothers, Joseph manages to catch up on the news back home. He learns that Jacob and Benjamin are still alive. He plays his big card when they mention Benjamin; on the pretense of checking out their story, he insists that Benjamin be brought down to Egypt. He then throws them all into jail for three days to think about it.

What Joseph is trying to learn is whether or not his brothers have really changed. Are they still the same villains who tried to get rid of him years before, or have they altered in their minds and hearts? He puts the pressure on them. He must find out. He finally shows them a bit of mercy (vv. 18–26).

In these encounters of Joseph with his brothers, there are two features to bear in mind:

First, Joseph understands everything they are saying among themselves, but the brothers, imagining that they are dealing with an Egyptian, do not know this. From their conversations, Joseph ascertains that they are still trying to deal with their ancient sin.

Joseph is joking at their expense and apparently having some fun at it. At the same time, however, he is hard hit by his own feelings as he sees what is happening to his brothers. Overcome with emotion, he must retire from the scene in order to weep.

Second, unlike his brothers, Joseph is aware how long the famine will last. He knows, therefore, that they will be back eventually. In order to guarantee it, he seizes Simeon, the second oldest. Joseph has just learned that the oldest, Reuben, had tried to save him at the time of his abduction; Reuben is spared.

Joseph puts a new twist on the game (vv. 27–28). His return of their money may seem like generosity on his part, but his brothers are terrified by it. It may appear, they fear, that they have run off without paying for their food, and this governor of Egypt is obviously no man to mess with. How could they ever explain how they had neglected to pay? We observe that Joseph does everything he can to keep his brothers off-balance. Within three chapters he will reduce them to quivering bundles of insecurity. Whatever arrogance or unrepentance or hardness of heart is still in them will be completely gone before Joseph is finished.

When the nine brothers arrive home (vv. 29–34), the whole story is told again, as a literary sort of "instant replay." This allows the reader to savor the irony of their situation. The brothers finish their account by breaking the really distressing news that Benjamin must accompany them on the next trip. This is too much for old Jacob (vv. 35–38), and now everybody is off-balance. Very protective of Benjamin, Jacob almost seems resigned to the loss of Simeon.

At this point, Reuben loses his mind, as it were, offering up Jacob's two grandsons. Joseph has certainly succeeded in throwing the whole family into a spin. Meanwhile, no matter what Jacob says, Joseph is quite certain that they will be back. After all, he knows just how long the famine will last. He holds all the good cards.

❦ Genesis 43 ❧

Eventually the family again runs short of food, so Jacob asks his sons to return to Egypt to procure some. The old man appears to be in a state of denial, giving the order as though there were no complications involved (vv. 1–2). It will be up to one of the older sons to remind him that things will not be so easy.

In the previous chapter it was Reuben who served as spokesman for the brothers, both to Joseph and to Jacob. As we saw, he had not been terribly successful, so this time Judah takes over the task (vv. 3–5). (The literary dynamics of this narrative, by the way, are destroyed by the modern hypothesis that postulates two "sources" here, ascribing chapter 42 to one source and chapter 43 to another. It is utterly pointless and without merit to speculate on hypothetical "sources" that do not exist and perhaps never existed. This sort of historical speculation is not only dubious in its impulse, it also constitutes a distraction from the literary enjoyment of the account.) Judah gives Jacob an ultimatum: Either risk Benjamin or the whole family will starve.

In response, Jacob goes from denial to blame (v. 6). His line of argument is, of course, futile. The point of no return was long ago reached. Jacob is dealing with a situation that no longer exists. Like many older people whose memories of the past are far more pleasant than the realities of the present, Jacob resists being reminded of the facts. The problem is that *he* is the one who must make the decision. His sons are powerless to do anything apart from his authority. They too, once again accused, become defensive (v. 7). Joseph had outwitted them; how could they have known? We readers understand, of course, but none of the participants up in Canaan have a clue.

Judah puts his foot down. Enough of this guilt, denial, and blame (vv. 8–10)! In his executive action, we perceive the attitude and skills of the kings to whom Judah will become the father: David, Solomon, Hezekiah, Josiah, Joseph of Nazareth. Judah obliges Jacob to give in (vv. 11–14), and the latter makes very practical suggestions about taking gifts to the Egyptian official and returning the money. Judah also assumes responsibility for Benjamin. Finally, he prays, not really knowing what he is praying for (though the reader knows), and not knowing that his prayer has already been answered.

The brothers return to Egypt (vv. 15–17). In their prior trip, Joseph had been rough with them. Now he is kind. What can it mean? So long receptive of bad news and not expecting anything different, the brothers are disposed to put an evil interpretation on the circumstances (vv. 18–22). The author of the passage is obviously relishing this description of their mounting anxiety. The brothers have wandered into the "big leagues," as it were. Faced with the grandeur of the Egyptian court, they fairly come undone. This "man" in Egypt is by far the most powerful person with whom they have ever dealt. They take their case to the head-steward who can speak to them in their own native tongue (v. 23). They never imagine that Joseph has understood everything they said before.

Once again, when the brothers meet Joseph, the prophecy in the ancient dream is fulfilled (vv. 24–26). Two dreams, two fulfillments. The reader begins to wonder how long Joseph can sustain this ongoing farce (vv. 27–30). He controls himself, however, for he still has one big test in mind, a final test. For a second time, nonetheless, Joseph is overcome with emotion.

During the meal, Joseph goes from this pathos to some more light kidding (vv. 31–34), placing his brothers at the table according to their ages, a fact that causes them some more consternation. Could this be an accident? This "man" in Egypt is most uncanny and mysterious. He holds them in the palm of his hand, as it were.

~ GENESIS 44 ~

We come now to the final test. As we saw in the two previous chapters, Joseph is hard put to control his emotions. He longs to reveal himself to his brothers. He must control himself, however, because there is a practical task to be accomplished. Being a practical man,

Joseph listens to his head more than his heart and prepares the final test (vv. 1–6).

After the departure of his brothers, he has them pursued (vv. 6–13). The brothers plead their innocence. With great confidence they offer the life of the guilty party if there be such a one among them. This is exactly what Jacob had said to Laban when the latter had complained about the theft of his household god (31:32). Once again the process goes by the oldest to the youngest, a procedure that permits the gradual build-up of suspense, reaching the climax of the scene in the discovery of the cup in Benjamin's sack.

The brothers at this point are struck silent. There is not a word, not an excuse, not a protestation. They now return to the city in silence, each man dealing privately with his own desperation. According to the terms of the steward, all of them may return safely home except Benjamin, but then they must face their father without Benjamin. Joseph has them exactly where he wants them. The trapdoor is closed. The brothers have run out of options. Now Joseph will learn what they are made of.

Joseph bears down on his brothers in inexorable, unbearable terms (vv. 14–17). At this point the author no longer speaks of "the brothers," but of "Judah and his brothers," a significant detail that serves to introduce Judah's lengthy speech that forms the second half of this chapter. We saw earlier that Judah has become the spokesman for the sons of Israel, their natural leader. It was he who endeavored to rescue Joseph in chapter 37, and the entire following chapter was devoted to him. He emerges now as the leader, who will become the father of Israel's kings.

As he begins his discourse (vv. 18–24), Judah stresses Jacob's special fondness for Benjamin. The reader notices that something has changed. Back when Joseph had been the favorite son, the rest of the brothers had been jealous. Now, however, they are not jealous of Benjamin. Now they are concerned with the welfare of their father, not their own. Judah continues (vv. 25–29), stressing how the old man would be distressed by the loss of his youngest son. He especially sets in parallel the earlier loss of Joseph and the now potential loss of Benjamin. This is the key. This is what Joseph must learn from his brothers. Will they treat Benjamin as they had, many years before, treated *him*? Will they permit Benjamin to become a slave, as they had, many years before, sold *him* into slavery? Will that great betrayal be repeated? Judah himself perceives that this is exactly his own moral situation. Will *he* repeat the former offense to their father? After all, the idea of selling Joseph into slavery had been Judah's (37:25–27).

Judah makes his final appeal, offering himself in slavery in place of his youngest brother (vv. 30–34). Judah will be the "substitute." Like his distant Descendant centuries later, he will make the atonement in the place of his brother. He will take upon himself his brother's offense, becoming the sacrificial victim to redeem the rest of the family. And he will do these things, like his distant Descendant many centuries later, out of love for his father. This is Judah's ultimate and compelling plea before the Throne: "The world must know that I love the Father" (John 14:31).

ᗰ GENESIS 45 ᗧ

The tension has been mounting for several chapters, as Joseph has, step by step, put to the test the spiritual state of his brothers. He has now utterly reduced them, forcing them to face their guilt and to assume responsibility for their plight. They are completely hopeless and limp before him. At the same time, Joseph has been obliged to place very tight, unnatural restraints on his own emotions, and now the latter have mounted to flood stage behind the restraining wall of his will. The time has come, then, to bring everything out into the open. No good will be served by further delay. Joseph speaks (vv. 1–3).

The brothers are not able to come to grips with the situation. This powerful stranger has suddenly started speaking to them in their own language. The veil is removed. If the brothers were vulnerable and despairing in the previous chapter, now things have become infinitely worse. They are now faced with a reality that they had not even slightly suspected. Joseph must repeat who he is (v. 4), and for the first time he mentions a little incident that happened in Dothan many years before. This reference can hardly provide comfort for the bewildered brothers, and Joseph must attempt to lessen their stark terror and anxiety (v. 5), for God's providence works even in sin (Philemon 15). God commands us always to meet evil with good, and God Himself models that commandment. Anyone can bring good from good. Divine activity is chiefly manifest in bringing good out of evil. Joseph must repeat the lesson to be learned (vv. 6–8).

Joseph alternates between practical concerns (vv. 9–13, 21–24) and more emotion stirred by the moment (vv. 14–15). If the brothers actually said anything at this point, it was probably incoherent. They become extremely passive and obedient. As long as they are in Egypt, chapter 45 will record not a single word from them. The entire impression from this chapter will be bewilderment to the point of stupefaction.

Joseph's single question to them has to do simply with his father. Like Judah in the previous chapter, Joseph's concern is with his father. This is entirely proper, because Jacob, on learning what has transpired, is overwhelmed with emotion (vv. 25–28). Some news is just too good to believe (compare Luke 24:37–38; Mark 16:9–13).

ᴄ: GENESIS 46 :~

The literary climax of the Joseph cycle has already occurred in the previous chapter. Now the story simply becomes a chronicle for a while. All that remains is for Jacob to die, thus finishing the narrative thread that has been relatively unattended for several chapters. This final part of Genesis chiefly prepares for Exodus.

Once again God reveals Himself to Jacob at Beersheba (vv. 1–4), as He has done each time Jacob moved, at Bethel (ch. 28) and at Peniel (ch. 32). God had also revealed Himself at Beersheba to Abraham (ch. 21) and Isaac (ch. 26). In that latter passage, as here in chapter 46, the message had to do with the great number of the promised posterity. Jacob now goes down into Egypt with few people, but they will be greatly multiplied over time. This is the latest in the series of migrations in Genesis, from Ur to Haran, from Haran to Canaan, from there to Mesopotamia, back down to Canaan, and now to Egypt (vv. 5–7).

There ensues a long list of those who went down into Egypt, their names preserved because these are the families who will form the company of the Exodus. These are, in short, the "first families" of the race. The list commences with the children of Leah (vv. 8–15), of which Levi's sons are of special importance, for theirs will be the genealogy of Israel's priesthood, including Moses and Aaron (vv. 11–12). The sons of Leah's handmaiden are listed next (vv. 16–18), followed by Rachel's children (vv. 19–22) and those of her handmaiden (vv. 23–26). The number "seventy" is a round number (cf. Acts 7:9–11).

Joseph is at last reunited to his father (vv. 28–30). The children of Israel were never to become sedentary in Egypt (vv. 31–34). They would never regard it as home.

⌁ GENESIS 47 ⌁

One discerns three stories in this chapter: (1) the movement of Jacob's family into Egypt (vv. 1–11); (2) Joseph's career as an Egyptian official (vv. 12–26); and (3) Jacob's burial request (vv. 27–31).

The first story has two scenes. First there is a scene involving Joseph's meeting Pharaoh with some of his brothers (vv. 1–5), and then a scene with Pharaoh and Jacob (vv. 5–11). (Since the two scenes are somewhat repetitious, it was inevitable that the textual reconstructionists would find two "sources" behind them.) In the first scene, care has been taken to relate the settlement of the family in Goshen to the earlier accounts of their nomadic life. The Egyptians, as the Sacred Text reminds us, were not fond of shepherds, an attitude reflecting the frequent strife between sedentary and nomadic peoples (a strife that goes back to Cain and Abel). The reference to Rameses in the second scene is anachronistic. The city did not acquire this name until the early thirteenth century before Christ, when Rameses II named it after himself. In verse 10 the verb "bless" should be preserved, as it is the best translation of the Hebrew *barak*. One recalls that "the lesser is blessed by the greater" (Hebrews 7:7). The patriarch really did bless the pharaoh; Jacob did not, as the New American Bible has it, simply "pay his respects" to Pharaoh. *Barak* is the same verb that will be used in the next chapter when Jacob blesses his grandsons.

In the second story (vv. 12–26) we see Joseph alter the entire economic and political structure of Egypt, not only saving the people in the time of famine, but also greatly strengthening the throne of Pharaoh. Indeed, it is not an exaggeration to say that what Joseph produced was a kind of servile welfare state, in which the government owned everything and taxes were high (twenty percent). The people even thanked him for it. (This detail is probably meant to be humorous. The writer is making fun of a people who, after being reduced to abject penury, are grateful for being taxed twenty percent. One also observes that Joseph, who has married into a clergy family, puts a clergy exemption into the tax code.) Eventually this economic and political situation would come back to haunt the Israelites, who would resent being slaves in a slave state. It would appear that Joseph himself created the servile conditions that would lead eventually to the Exodus.

In the third story (vv. 27–31), Jacob, making it clear that Egypt is not the family's real home, arranges to be buried in the Promised Land (cf. Hebrews 11:21). The exact meaning of the text, with respect to Jacob's gesture, has been unclear almost from the beginning. Originally it may have meant only that he nodded assent on his pillow.

⁓ Genesis 48 ⁓

Because of his special role in saving the family, Joseph receives something like the blessing of the firstborn—that is, a double portion; he became the father of two of Israel's tribes. That meant that his descendants would settle twice the amount of the Promised Land as any of his brothers. Ephrem and Manasseh became, as it were, the sons of Israel himself (vv. 1–7).

When Jacob is introduced to the two boys (vv. 8–11), his poor eyesight reminds us of aging Isaac, of whose blindness Jacob had taken advantage. The irony is striking. In that earlier case too the larger blessing had been given to the younger son. What Isaac had done by mistake, however, Jacob will do on purpose (vv. 12–15). A Christian reader will take note of Jacob's *crossing* of his hands in the act of blessing. It is noteworthy that at least one Christian reader of this text referred to this action as an act of "faith" (Hebrews 11:21, the only example of faith that this epistle ascribes to Jacob). In the blessing itself (vv. 15–16), Jacob reaches back two generations in order to reach forward two generations.

Joseph, though he governs Egypt, is unable to govern his old father (vv. 17–20). Jacob, let it be said, knew a thing or two about blessings: "I know, my son, I know." Jacob has been reversing everything since the day he was born, right after tripping up his older brother as the latter emerged from the womb (25:22–23). Right to the end of his life he continues to take the side of the younger man. It is a trait of his personality.

⌒: GENESIS 49 :⌒

It has long been noticed that some of the imagery of this chapter seems to be based on figures in the Babylonian zodiac. The number of Jacob's sons, twelve, lent itself readily to the imagery of a zodiac. (This will also be true of the Bible's last book, where the symbolisms of Jacob's twelve sons will be combined with the symbolisms of the twelve apostles. Zodiacal imagery is found everywhere in the Book of Revelation.) That Babylonian zodiac, like all solar zodiacs, had twelve "signs," some of which were identical to the later Greek and Roman zodiacs. Indeed, in the present chapter we find the images of Aquarius (v. 4), Gemini (v. 5), Leo (v. 9), and Sagittarius (v. 23). Other images in this chapter are not found in the later zodiacs, however, such as the ass, the serpent, the hind, the colt, and the wolf.

Reuben does not fare too well in the blessing (vv. 3–4), because of his sin (35:22). His tribe evaporated, as it were, rather early in Israel's history, absorbed by the other tribes and by the Syrians. In the final list of the tribes it will appear second, after Judah (Revelation 7:5). Like Reuben, Simeon and Levi (vv. 5–7) would cease to exist as political entities. Simeon would be absorbed by Judah, and Levi, as the priestly tribe, would be divided up among all the others as a special class without specific tribal territory. Neither tribe will show up in the roll in Judges 5, and in the final blessing of Moses, in Deuteronomy 33, Simeon is not mentioned at all. In short, a certain cloud hangs over Jacob's three oldest sons, whose tribes are displaced in seniority by the royal tribe, the family of Judah (vv. 8–12).

Flavius Josephus tells us that Jacob lived seventeen years in

Egypt (*Antiquities* 2.8.1). The biblical description of Jacob's death (vv. 28–33) is remarkable for its failure to mention death! Jacob simply goes "to his people" (*el-'ammiw*). Jacob had become Israel, and Israel had become a people. Hence, it was deemed inappropriate to come right out and say that Jacob had died. Jacob was Israel, and Israel still lived.

❦ GENESIS 50 ❧

This chapter has three parts: (1) the burial of Jacob (vv. 1–14), (2) Joseph and his brothers (vv. 15–21), and (3) the death and burial of Joseph (vv. 22–26).

Egyptian embalming was one of the great curiosities of the ancient world, a feature that made Egypt famous. Whereas modern techniques of embalming are designed to disguise the effects of death for only a short time, Egyptian mummification was an attempt to resist the effects of death as much as possible, an endeavor to defy permanently the decay and corruption of the body. Jacob's embalming required forty days (vv. 1–6). By Egyptian standards, this was pretty short. Ancient Egyptian texts suggest something closer to seventy days, which is the number of mourning days indicated in verse 3. The large retinue of Jacob's funeral cortege (vv. 7–9) serves to stress his prestige and importance. The site of his burial (vv. 10–14) ties this story back to the earlier accounts in the patriarchal narrative. This property had been "in the family" ever since Abraham purchased it in chapter 23 as the family burial plot. Sarah, we recall, was the first to be buried there.

This later account of Joseph and his brothers (vv. 15–21) continues a theme from chapter 45. We contrast the magnanimity of Joseph with the pettiness of the pitiful brothers, who were trying to save their necks with a very thin fabrication. Josephus places this story up in the land of Canaan, immediately after Jacob's burial. He says that the brothers were fearful of returning to Egypt with Joseph.

The reference to Joseph's "brothers" at his burial (vv. 22–26) should be interpreted simply to mean his relatives, which is the normal meaning of the word "brother" in Holy Scripture. Joseph was, after all, younger than most of his blood brothers. Stephen's sermon seems to indicate that *all* of Jacob's sons were buried at Shechem (Acts 7:16). In the rabbinical tradition, however, that site was Hebron (cf. Josephus, *Antiquities* 2.8.2).

Excursus:

Providence, Christology, & the Resurrection

The Joseph story is an example of what we may call a "secular," as distinct from a "sacral," narrative. That is to say, except for the dreams and their interpretation, there are no miraculous events in the account, no stupendous irruptions of the divine into the human, nor any sacred setting, such as an apparition or a supernatural locution. God does not explicitly enter the story as an actor; the divine activity is entirely behind the scenes. God performs His wonders through people. There is no obvious and extraordinary "break" into what otherwise appears to be an account of human activity. There is no miraculous healing, no pillar of fire, no burning bush, no rods turned into snakes nor water into wine. Except that the chief character is unusually astute, wise, and discerning, even to the point of reading dreams, the elements in the account simply unfold in a natural and normal way. God is certainly active, but the reader never knows exactly how.

While God's direction of events in the Joseph account consists in the providential oversight of human activity, we also note a special emphasis on the divine management, as it were, even of sinful activity. This story is a fine illustration of God's ability to bring good from evil. So the wise and forgiving Joseph can announce to his sinful brothers, "Now therefore, do not be grieved or angry with yourselves because you sold me here; for God sent me before you to save life" (45:5; also v. 7), and later, "But as for you, you meant evil against me; but God meant it for good" (50:20).

The story of Joseph, then, is an account of Divine Providence. Its clear thesis consists in the proposition that "all things work together for good to those who love God" (Romans 8:28). In everything that happens to Joseph, God is "with" him (Genesis 39:3, 5, 21–23). This affirmation of Divine Providence in the Joseph story is not only implied in the text but also made explicit by its chief character.

Moreover, Joseph's insights into God's working in history are explicitly regarded as coming from the Holy Spirit (in 41:38), reminding us that the general affirmation in Romans 8:28 also is contextualized by the theology of the Holy Spirit and especially by the principle that "as many as are led by the Spirit of God, these are sons of God" (Romans 8:14).

This faithful reliance on God's providential guidance of history is the secret of Joseph's inner life. It explains both his patience in tribulation and his ready forgiveness of enemies. Even as a slave, even in prison, Joseph was an inwardly free man (Cyril of Alexandria, *In Joannem* 5.8.36). He was perpetually and prayerfully mindful of the presence of God (Procopius of Gaza, *In Genesim* 50).

Following the lead of the Fathers and the ancient liturgies of the Church, however, we are not content to interpret Joseph purely in his Old Testament setting. The Tradition of the Church, the same Tradition that canonized the books of the Bible, provides a further hermeneutic context: the Mystery of Christ and the Church's life in Christ. Here must Joseph ultimately be understood.

In that context Joseph is perceived, not only as a prophet, but also as a prophecy. As early as Tertullian, Joseph was regarded as a figure (*figuravit . . . figuratus*) of Christ Himself (*Adversus Judaeos* 10; *Adversus Marcionem* 3.18), and Cyprian called him a "type of Christ" (*Testimonia* 1.20; cf. also his

De Laude Martyrii 29).This view was shared by Fathers both East (Cyril of Alexandria, Sophronius of Jerusalem, Germanus of Constantinople) and West (Ambrose, Augustine, Gregory Dialogos).

Sometimes the particulars perceived in that typology are less than impressive. It was observed early, for example, that both Joseph and Jesus began their public ministries at about age thirty (Origen, *In Matthaeum*, "Series" 78). Likewise, the fact that Joseph was alive when thought to be dead made him seem a symbol of the risen Christ (Rufinus, *Benedictio Joseph* 2).

Far more significant, however, is the perception of Joseph as a type of Christ in the setting of the Passion. The Eastern Church in particular has long read the Joseph story during Holy Week, a context highlighting so many resemblances of Joseph to Jesus: the beloved of his father, sold for a price by his brethren, unjustly accused and imprisoned on false testimony, suffering all with patience, and finally showing mercy towards his oppressors. Joseph's life thus outlined those dramatic days culminating on Calvary. Such is the contemplative vision enshrined forever in the Matins Bridegroom Service of Holy Week in the Orthodox Church:"Joseph is an image of the Master: he was thrown into a pit and sold by his brethren, but he suffered all these things with patience, as a true figure of Christ."

Joseph probably did not seem so far away to the early Church Fathers as he does to us. His tomb at Shechem was yet known in the third century and venerated by the Samaritans who lived there (Origen, *In Joannem* 13.26). It was still being visited more than two centuries later (Jerome, *Quaestiones in Genesim* 48).

That grave was the special possession of Shechem, the ancient tribal center of Manasseh and the scene of the covenantal renewal under Joshua: "And the bones of Joseph, which the sons of Israel had brought up out of Egypt, they buried at Shechem in a plot of ground that Jacob had purchased from the sons of Hamor for a hundred silver pieces" (Joshua 24:32). Doubtless it was at Shechem that Israel of old had chiefly narrated the epic charge of the dying Joseph to his relatives:

> Then Joseph said to his brethren, "I am about to die; but God will surely visit you, and bring you out of this land to the land God swore to our fathers, Abraham, Isaac, and Jacob." Thus Joseph took an oath from the children of Israel, saying, "God will surely visit you, and you shall carry up my bones from here." So Joseph died, being one hundred and ten years old; and they embalmed him, and put him in a coffin in Egypt. (50:24–26)

Joseph's declaration was a prophecy of the Exodus (John Chrysostom, *Homiliae in Genesim* 67.5). Moreover, because of the steps he took to ensure that his very bones would be part of that salvific event, the hurried actions of Passover night included the opening of Joseph's grave: "Now Moses took the bones of Joseph with him, for he had placed the children of Israel under solemn oath, saying, 'God will surely visit you, and you shall carry up my bones from here with you'" (Exodus 13:19).

Those bones are not mentioned again until their burial at Shechem, but the attentive imagination is fascinated by their being borne from place to place over the next forty years, completing the entire journey through the desert, over the dry bed of the Jordan and into the Promised Land, a sustained thread linking the Patriarchs, the Exodus, Sinai, and the Conquest.

In rabbinical tradition this singular treatment of Joseph's body was a special mark of his dignity. According to the Mishnah, "who is greater to us than Joseph, with whom none other than Moses concerned himself? Moses merited the bones of Joseph, and no one in Israel is greater than he" ("Sota" 1.9).

Joseph normally was mentioned when the People of God took the roll call of its heroes (Wisdom 10:13f; 1 Maccabees 2:53; 4 Maccabees 18:11; Acts 7:9–16; Clement of Rome 4.9). Therefore, it is not surprising to find him in the narrative tabulation of Hebrews 11: "By faith Joseph, when he was dying, made mention of the departure of the children of Israel, and gave instructions concerning his bones" (v. 22). It is curious that, with so many examples of faith to choose from in the history of Joseph, the author of Hebrews should content himself with this one instance. I believe, however, that Hebrews 11:22 tells the whole story of Joseph's bones from a specifically Christian perspective: death and the Exodus. It was in the very act of dying, *teleuton*, that Joseph spoke of the Exodus.

Throughout Hebrews 11 faith constantly is related to death; death is *the* test of faith. While this truth is clearest in the instances of Abel (v. 4), Enoch (v. 5), Abraham (vv. 17f), Jacob (v. 21), Moses' parents (v. 23), and the later witnesses (vv. 32–39), it is also implied in the cases of Noah (v. 7), Sarah (v. 12), Isaac (v. 20) and Moses (vv. 25f). In the Epistle to the Hebrews, faith has to do with how one dies, and "these all died in faith" (v. 13).

To the author of Hebrews, then, Joseph offered the ideal model of how a Christian should die—clinging in hope to the promise of the Exodus. The very word *exodos*, departure, was sometimes used as a euphemism for death. Its very specific Old Testament use and reference, however, provided Christians with a special way of describing death, relating it to the Cross and to Jesus' entire passing to the Father. As the death of Jesus was spoken of in terms of Exodus (Luke 9:31) and Passover (1 Corinthians 5:7), so too was the death of Christians: "knowing that shortly I must put off my tent, just as our Lord Jesus Christ showed me. Moreover I will be careful to ensure that you always have a reminder of these things after my decease [exodos]" (2 Peter 1:14f).

Moreover, the reference to the Exodus in Hebrews 11:22 is completely consonant with its subsequent context. Verses 23–29 speak of the Passover and the Red Sea, and verse 28 specifically refers to the blood of the paschal lamb. The author is here touching on an ancient Christian catechetical pattern that linked the Exodus and Passover to the events surrounding the death and Resurrection of Jesus by interpretive paradigm and type.

For the author of Hebrews this participation of Joseph's body in Israel's deliverance points to a particular dimension of the Christian faith. It indicates the hope that our very bodies are destined for passage through the real Red Sea and a final rest in the real Promised Land. The real Exodus is the Resurrection. The God who can raise the dead (Hebrews 11:19) has already "brought up our Lord Jesus from the dead" (Hebrews 13:20).

Joseph was confident that his original burial in Genesis 50:26 was a temporary arrangement, for he knew that his body would eventually leave Egypt and go to the Promised Land. In holding such a confidence, he is well regarded as a symbol and type of the Christian hope. Theologically speaking, after all, we Christians do not "own" our sepulchers; we borrow them from Christ, somewhat as He borrowed His from Joseph of Arimathea. Jesus holds the very mortgage on our tombs. Our sanctified bodies are not cast out from His presence; they are laid to rest in Akel Dama, the burial ground of strangers, "the field of the Blood," that sacred plot purchased at so high a price.

Contrary to the assertions of countless preachers, then, it is not the function of a Christian funeral to put someone in his *"final* resting place." On the contrary, the very wording of a Christian funeral should go out of its way to emphasize that burial itself is a purely temporary housing arrangement.

In the last words spoken over an Eastern Orthodox Christian when he is laid in the ground, the Church explicitly affirms: "The *Lord's* is the earth, and the fullness thereof—the world and all that it contains." This is our final affirmation that "Jesus is Lord"; namely, that He is the Lord of the land, the true Landlord, proprietor of the real estate bought with His Blood. And affirmed in that proclamation is the godly guarantee that this Landlord will duly serve eviction notices on us all, on that final day when Israel goes forth from Egypt and the house of Jacob from a people of alien tongue.

ABOUT THE AUTHOR

Patrick Henry Reardon is pastor of All Saints Antiochian Orthodox Church in Chicago, Illinois, and Senior Editor of *Touchstone: A Journal of Mere Christianity.*

Ancient Faith Publishing hopes you have enjoyed and benefited from this book. The proceeds from the sales of our books only partially cover the costs of operating our nonprofit ministry—which includes both the work of **Ancient Faith Publishing** (formerly known as Conciliar Press) and the work of **Ancient Faith Radio.** Your financial support makes it possible to continue this ministry both in print and online. Donations are tax-deductible and can be made at www.ancientfaith.com.

To request a catalog of other publications,
please call us at (800) 967-7377 or (219) 728-2216
or log onto our website: **store.ancientfaith.com**

 ANCIENT FAITH RADIO

Bringing you Orthodox Christian music, readings, prayers,
teaching, and podcasts 24 hours a day since 2004 at
www.ancientfaith.com

ALSO BY PATRICK HENRY REARDON

The Trial of Job:
Orthodox Christian Reflections on the Book of Job

"What Fr. Patrick Reardon achieves with this book is to render Job comprehensible (to those of us who are still lay readers of Scripture), tangible (to those who have not yet tasted the way of darkness and despair), and accessible (to those who have already experienced any form of brokenness and broken-heartedness). Ultimately, all of us identify with one or another aspect of Job's life. As life inevitably informs and as this book intuitively confirms, one cannot sing Psalms without having read Job!"—Fr. John Chryssavgis, Author of *Light Through Darkness* and *Soul Mending* Paperback, 112 pages (ISBN 978-1-888212-72-3)

Chronicles of History and Worship:
Orthodox Christian Reflections on the Books of Chronicles

The Old Testament Books of Chronicles contain some of the most neglected passages in all of Scripture. Understanding their message can be a difficult and daunting task for the modern reader. Popular writer and Old Testament scholar Patrick Reardon brings these important books to life, unfolding their powerful message for our own day and age.

Like any family history, the story of Chronicles is told with a distinct purpose in mind. It asks the question: "What was the real and lasting significance of King David and his house?" Beginning with the long list of names of the first chapter, this heritage is revealed in cosmic significance. It has in fact become the family tree of every true believer.
Paperback, 188 pages (ISBN: 978-1-888212-83-9)

Wise Lives
Orthodox Christian Reflections on the Wisdom of Sirach

Sirach concentrates on the practical application of the fear of God to daily life, but also gives attention to the role of biography and historical literature in the shaping of the soul.
Paperback, 180 pages (ISBN: 978-0-982270-3-4)

Christ in the Psalms

A highly inspirational book of meditations on the Psalms by one of the most insightful and challenging Orthodox writers of our day. Avoiding both syrupy sentimentality and arid scholasticism, *Christ in the Psalms* takes the reader on a thought-provoking and enlightening pilgrimage through this beloved "Prayer Book" of the Church.

Which psalms were quoted most frequently in the New Testament, and how were they interpreted? How has the Church historically understood and utilized the various psalms in her liturgical life? How can we perceive the image of Christ shining through the psalms? Lively and highly devotional, thought-provoking yet warm and practical, *Christ in the Psalms* sheds a world of insight upon each psalm, and offers practical advice for how to make the Psalter a part of our daily lives. Paperback, 328 pages (ISBN 978-1-888212-21-7)

Christ in His Saints

In this sequel to *Christ in the Psalms,* Patrick Henry Reardon once again applies his keen intellect to a topic he loves most dearly. Here he examines the lives of almost one hundred and fifty saints and heroes from the Scriptures—everyone from Abigail to Zephaniah, Adam to St. John the Theologian. This well-researched work is a veritable cornucopia of Bible personalities: Old Testament saints, New Testament saints, "Repentant saints," "Zealous saints," "Saints under pressure" . . . they're all here, and their stories are both fascinating and uplifting.

But *Christ in His Saints* is far more than just a biblical who's who. These men and women represent that ancient family into which, by baptism, all believers have been incorporated. Together they compose that great "cloud of witnesses" cheering us on and inspiring us through word and deed. Paperback, 320 pages (ISBN 978-1-888212-68-6)

To request a catalog of other books about the Orthodox Faith and church life, to place a credit card order, or to obtain current ordering information, please call Ancient Faith Publishing at (800) 967-7377 or (219) 728-2216, or go to our website: store.ancientfaith.com.

Visit ancientfaith.com to listen to podcasts by Patrick Henry Reardon.

CPSIA information can be obtained
at www.ICGtesting.com
Printed in the USA
FSHW010632031019

9 781888 212969